One Thing I Ask...

One Thing I Ask…

Praying God's Heart Through His Word

Debbie Howell

My Editors:
Grace Brown and Chris Howell

"The word *Shalom* is derived from one of the names of God. It is the Hebrew root word for *complete* or *whole* according to the Torah and is often symbolized by the dove."

-By Roger Preston, Book Cover Artist

Library of Congress Control Number:		2016902304
ISBN:	Hardcover	978-1-5144-5973-7
	Softcover	978-1-5144-5972-0
	eBook	978-1-5144-6722-0

Scriptures marked as "(CEV)" are taken from the *Contemporary English Version* Copyright © 1995 by *American Bible Society*. Used by permission.

Scripture quotations marked AMP are from *The Amplified Bible*, Old Testament copyright © 1965, 1987 by the *Zondervan* Corporation. *The Amplified Bible*, New Testament copyright © 1954, 1958, 1987 by *The Lockman Foundation*. Used by permission. All rights reserved.

Scripture quotations marked NIV are taken from the *Holy Bible, New International Version*. *NIV*. Copyright © 1973, 1978, 1984 by International Bible Society. Used by permission of *Zondervan*. All rights reserved. [*Biblica*]

Any people depicted in stock imagery provided by Thinkstock are models, and such images are being used for illustrative purposes only.
Certain stock imagery © Thinkstock.

Print information available on the last page.

Rev. date: 03/18/2016

To order additional copies of this book, contact:
Xlibris
1-888-795-4274
www.Xlibris.com
Orders@Xlibris.com
735887

"One Thing I Ask" is an inviting, refreshing, encouraging, inspirational book for any Christian who is looking to develop, grow deeper in, or re-ignite their relationship with God through His Word. This how-to-book filled with powerful scriptures throughout begins each chapter with the author's riveting personal testimony of her Christian journey & real-life experiences and ends with teachings on relevant & practical ways to incorporate and make God's Word a personal part of one's everyday life. This book is perfect for any Christian who hungers to know God more intimately & is searching for a more fulfilling relationship with God than ever before!—Renée Rucker

"One Thing I Ask" is a fresh, inspiring, honest and relevant way to approach and apply God's Word. I love all the practical applications from the author's real-life experiences and the detailed examples of how to incorporate them into daily life. This is a must read for anyone desiring to start a spiritual journey or if you feel stuck and need to press the restart button. I have fallen in love once again with my Creator and feel spiritually reenergized and ready to tackle whatever comes my way by reading this inspirational book.—Georgina Straw

This is a great book on the joys and burdens of living a prayer filled life. Debbie relates experiences with Chris, her husband, and her two daughters, Jasmine and Camilia. She is not afraid to tell of disappointment as well as success. It will inspire each reader to a deeper experience with Jesus Christ.—Pr. David Newman

"One Thing I Ask" will inspire you to open your heart to the faithfulness of God. As I began to read, each chapter spoke to me about who God is and it reminded me of who I am in Him. This book encourages you to find scripture that will help support you on your journey with God, enabling you to connect with Him on a deeper level. Thank you, Debbie for being vulnerable enough to share moments where God has impacted your life greatly.—Michelle Nelson

Debbie takes the reader on a heartfelt journey of finding prayer's true power and efficacy for your life and a renewed meaning and purpose in your study. She shares personal stories of her God moments when the fragility of her humanity connected with the might of divinity. You will see through every chapter of these God moments how He reveals His love, grace, and power where the answers in His Word meet her heartfelt prayers. Through her helpful tips on "Practicing the Word" your devotional life and study will be rejuvenated. Your faithful prayers will take on new meaning and purpose. Life's journey is rife with God moments. Moments on the journey where people experience such emptiness that God pours overflowing amounts of His presence of love, peace, and grace into their lives. Take the journey "One Thing I Ask" and be renewed by the power of prayerful practice of the Word.—Brian Wright *(Briteradio.org)*

CONTENTS

INTRODUCTION

PEOPLE ARE HURTING. And whether it's leading a ministry, singing on a praise team, or now writing my first book, God's call always comes from a need. He will open the eyes of my heart to hurting people, then tell me that He's calling me to love them in His name. This is the way that God has consistently called and used me.

There's a great need in this world to hear from God. Even Christians who go to church faithfully have times of frustration when they need to hear God's voice and don't know how to make it happen. For the last 10 years God has been revealing to me the path to knowing Him, hearing His voice, and being confident that my life is mirroring His will.

Even now, as I pray for guidance, my heart is breaking as I'm communicating with my Uncle LaVerne, who has been struggling emotionally for years since he fought in the Vietnam War. How do you find God when there's deep-rooted pain that manifests itself in nightmares every time you close your eyes? Where is the power that flowed from Jesus so naturally and consistently?

What I've come to discover is that God's answer, His will, His very presence, can be found in His Word. Without delving into the heart of this book prematurely, let me say that all we have to do is study how God-fearing men and women and even Jesus Himself connected with God through His Word, and we would be inspired to meet God there every day.

As I write this book I am driven by a great passion to get heart-to-heart with God. And as my intimacy with Him grows through my time in His Word, my desire also fuels my urgency to share with you what is being revealed to me.

My prayer is that as I share my story with you that God's Word would penetrate deep into your heart (Prov. 4:20-22). It's time to contemplate His beauty and study at His feet (Psalm 27:4).

CHAPTER 1

"If I Only Knew Then"

Psalm 27 (CEV)
4 I ask only one thing, Lord:
  Let me live in your house
  every day of my life
  to see how wonderful you are
  and to pray in your temple.
8 My heart tells me to pray.
  I am eager to see your face,
14 Trust the Lord!
  Be brave and strong
  and trust the Lord.

IN 1991 MY husband, Chris, and I graduated from college and moved to Africa as missionaries. We lived and worked at a school located deep in the bush on a remote and beautiful campus. I worked as a teacher at the school and some of my favorite classes were held during the summer months. During these summer sessions I taught adult students who were already working in their respective fields, but had not yet completed their education. I was only in my early 20s and most of them were older than me. In spite of this, I loved teaching and getting to know them. I remember so clearly one day when we were having a discussion in class, one of the older students (I'm guessing he may have been close to 60) opened up and shared his struggle as a Christian, because tribal hatred ran deep in his heart. He shared that from the time he was a very young boy he was taught to hate people from certain other tribes, and he didn't know how to overcome it. I felt his pain and we all talked about this issue that so many people in that country faced. I really appreciated his honesty and was in total shock when I heard what happened only a few weeks later. That same student was in the capital city for a meeting. He was sitting around a table with several other men, some of whom were from other tribes. The discussion became heated and he leapt across the table with a knife, fully intending to stab another man. Praise God that his plans were thwarted, but that really shook me up. I somehow felt partially responsible as his teacher. he had reached out, but I was unable to help him receive the power of God for his breakthrough.

If we really believe in an all-powerful God, believing not with our heads, but with our hearts that He really did perform all of those incredible miracles throughout the Bible, then where is He now? Quite frankly, some of us would be happy if He would just tell us which job to take or heal the headaches (literally and figuratively) that won't seem to go away. But isn't there so much more?

Lloyd John Ogilvie, one of my favorite writers, taps into the answer to this question. He writes, "Knowing the fact that God can make things happen is of little help until we know him personally" ("The Bush is Still Burning," p.18).

The answer then comes in what, for me, is one of the most powerful chapters in the Bible. When the Holy Spirit began to shed light on Psalm 119 into my heart, I became so excited! This chapter (which, not surprisingly, is the longest in the Bible) is David's secret to not only how he defeated Goliath, but also to how closely he lived heart-to-heart with God.

Once you learn how to listen to God through His Word, it becomes like an amazing treasure hunt. There are so many incredible things that He cannot wait to share with you that are like diamonds hidden deep within the ground.

Let me share with you some of my favorite verses from Psalm 119.

"I seek You with my whole heart... Your Word have I hid in my heart that I might not sin against You" (v. 10-11).

DEBBIE HOWELL

"Open my eyes so I can see wonderful truths in Your law" (v. 18).

"Your testimonies are my delight, they guide me in the way I should live" (v. 24).

"My soul is burdened down with worry; lift me up with Your Word" (v. 28).

"I take comfort in what You have said, because Your Word gives me hope" (v. 50).

"My trust in Your Word strengthened me" (v. 81).

"Oh Lord, I love Your law; I meditate on it all day long" (v. 97).

"Your Word is a light for my feet, and You help me see a path in the dark" (v. 105).

"I remain awake through the different hours of the night meditating on the promises of Your Word" (v. 148).

"I rejoice in Your Scriptures like someone finding a great treasure" (v. 162).

"Help me to understand what is in Your Word" (v. 169).
(all from The Prayer Bible, A Modern Translation)

Once you begin to unpack David's relationship with God through His Word, it brings new meaning to how he faced and defeated Goliath in 1 Samuel 17. Verse 48 says that David ran toward Goliath "in the Name of the Lord of the Heavens, the God of Israel." David was angry because of what Goliath was saying about his God. Have you ever felt enraged because someone said something offensive about one of your family members or a close friend? Your gut instinct is to stand up for the one who means so much to you and to stop their reputation from being ruined. That's what is so amazing about David's relationship with God. It was so real and personal that he couldn't stand to hear bad things said about his God and he would bring down any giant who was defaming the name of his friend.

Another part of this story that really inspires me is that David's self-proclaimed victory is yet another secret to his success. He proclaimed *who* his God is! He was in essence saying, "Listen, you giant, do you have any idea who you are talking about here? He is the Lord of even the heavens! You mess with Him and I'll mess with you! This is the same God Who gave me the power to kill a lion and a bear and guess what? By His power, in His great Name, He will now help me defeat you!"

I heard something very interesting recently. It was part of a prayer by a close friend of mine, Pastor Ann Roda. As we were praying together, she prayed that we would use the Word of God as our "filter" as we pray. She was in essence saying that we should pray through Who God is in His Word. Because of the amazing things God has been teaching me, that little phrase jumped right into my spirit. That's exactly what David did. He may have run toward his Goliath with tenacity and boldness, but you know that young boy was sending up prayers like we shoot out text messages!

There are so many things I could share about David's Goliath-defeating story, but one thing I urgently want to communicate to you right now is that if you want your prayers to be filled with power, if you want to know with certainty that God hears you when you pray, then it is essential that we KNOW the God whom we pray to! Just like David, when you say God's Name, it should evoke an intimacy in your heart that leaves no room for doubt when you pray.

Practicing the Word

One of my favorite things to do with Psalm 119 is to pray it while replacing David's name with my own. I'll unpack this process more in later chapters, but for now I encourage you to put this book down, pick up your favorite translation of the Bible (or go to *Biblegateway.com*) and spend some time getting to know the God of David in Psalm 119. Next, grab a journal or notebook and write out the verses that speak to you and write down a personal Scripture prayer.

For example, "God please open my eyes so I can see wonderful truths in Your law (18). Oh Lord, I love Your law; I meditate on it all day long (97). I rejoice in Your Scriptures like someone finding a great treasure (162). Help me to understand what is in Your Word" (169).

CHAPTER 2

"I Was My Own Bully"

Psalm 27 (AMP)

4 One thing I have asked of the Lord, and that I will seek:
    That I may dwell in the house of the Lord [in His presence]
    all the days of my life,
    To gaze upon the beauty [the delightful loveliness and
    majestic grandeur] of the Lord
    And to meditate in His temple.

8 When You said, "Seek My face [in prayer, require My
    presence as your greatest need]," my heart said to You,
    "Your face, O Lord, I will seek [on the authority of Your
    word]."

14 Wait for and confidently expect the Lord;
    Be strong and let your heart take courage;
    Yes, wait for and confidently expect the Lord.

WE ALL HAVE people whom we deeply care about in this world. Countless prayers go up to Heaven on behalf of those we love. As I mentioned earlier, God has been teaching me a lot about prayer, and one of His platforms for these lessons has been my heart's cry regarding my older daughter, Jasmine. When she turned 14 things changed drastically in our home. This wasn't one of those typical "teenage rebellion has entered our nice quiet home" stories. I believe that my father's unexpected death led to some dark times for Jasmine, since she didn't know how to properly grieve. By the time we realized the struggle she was in, she was into dark websites and music and was cutting herself for emotional relief. We found ourselves in panic mode.

We talked with her, even pled with her to the point of tears, but she would not be moved.

I don't remember how it all started, just that I had been reading some powerful Christian books and listening to a lot of Joyce Meyer's (Christian motivational speaker) sermons. God began responding to my efforts of seeking Him. He began throwing beams of light in my direction and prompting me to find verses in His Word to pray over my daughter.

One particular story comes to mind during that time. I was reading a powerful book by a Christian author, and as I began reading a certain page I felt impressed to ask Jasmine to read it. I knew she wouldn't be excited about the idea, but I was learning that an important part of hearing the voice of God is obeying when He speaks. She was in her bedroom so I opened the door, told her that God wanted her to read the page I had marked, and leaving the book on her desk, I quietly retreated. I remember the next day wanting my book back so I could continue reading it, but the Holy Spirit lovingly said, "Don't even think about it!" A couple of nights later I was lying in bed, struggling to trust God with Jasmine instead of giving in to panicked thoughts about her. God was teaching me the importance of believing His Word over my circumstances and feelings. As I lay in bed, God reminded me of a Scripture that I had written out regarding her: "He gives blessings to His beloved in their sleep" (Psalm 127:2).

So to fight off my panic, I lay in bed praying that Scripture, "God You give blessings to Your beloved in their sleep. Thank you God that You give me blessings when I sleep. You are calling me to receive Your blessings instead of panic. I receive Your blessings, God, even as I sleep." I fell asleep meditating on that Scripture, only to be awakened later that night by Jasmine. With tears in her eyes, she said she needed to talk to me. I followed her into her room and she said, "Mom, I want to talk to you about the book you left in my room. It's been sitting there for a couple of days and I had no intention of reading it. But God wouldn't leave me alone about it, so out of frustration I finally picked it up. Mom, as I began reading the page you marked, it was as if God Himself entered my room. I don't know how to explain it, but He is real."

That was one of many experiences that Jasmine had with God as I continued to obey Him and pray Scripture over her instead of giving in to fear. It wasn't an overnight breakthrough, because He won't force Himself on us, but He will definitely make His presence known, and after two years of God encounters Jasmine chose His light over the darkness she had been in.

Jasmine is now 21 and her battle is not over. There's a depression that lingers and there have been times when I've been tempted to say, "Well, there's no hope in praying anymore. God hasn't answered and apparently He never will." This book is not being written from the Promised Land — I'm still on the journey. I'm still holding on, still believing, and still learning Who God is. But my focus has now changed. When I sit down with God in His Word, it's not about finding that "magic" Scripture that will be the perfect fit for my need. I am all about knowing God now. I love my time with Him. I love the fact that I can pray Scriptures through the filter of Who He is: Love. I don't have to worry about when or how He will answer. If I had to choose whether my prayer time will accomplish answered prayers or knowing God, I would choose to know God. I can understand with a greater appreciation what Paul meant in Philippians 3:8 "I count everything as loss compared to the possession of the priceless privilege (the overwhelming preciousness, the surpassing worth, and supreme advantage) of knowing Christ Jesus my Lord and of progressively becoming more deeply and intimately acquainted with Him [of perceiving and recognizing and understanding Him more fully and clearly]."

Growing in faith. It isn't easy sometimes. I've been confessing Scripture over Jasmine for a long time as I've seen the ups and downs of her depression. But God rewards those who diligently seek Him and there are always rays of light along the way. Just recently, I was with her, going to help her choose her fall college classes, when the light of Heaven hit my car. My girl started sharing with me amazing things God has been teaching her. She had recently spoken with two different Christian counselors and something about their combined advice gave her a God moment. She shared with me (after cautioning me to save my "praise God hallelujah service" until we got out of the car!) that she realized she has been her own bully. The devil has been flinging self-hatred thoughts at her for years and she has been not only letting him get away with it, but also agreeing with him! She said, "Mom, there were even times when I tried to listen to Christian music, but I would start feeling so angry that I had to turn it off. I now realize that Satan didn't want any positive thoughts in my mind so he stirred up anger in me." To hear Jasmine say how important it is for her to think and verbalize Scriptures and positive words and even to sing out praises to God made my faith in God absolutely soar! It reminded me of the Scripture verses that God had been leading me to pray over her.

"Jasmine is not giving up. How could she! Even though on the outside it often looks like things are falling apart on her, on the inside, where God is making new life, not a day goes by without His unfolding grace" (2 Corinthians 4:1).

"Jasmine is content to be herself, her life will count for plenty" (Matthew 23:12).

There have even been times when God's Word was fulfilled so specifically in her life that there was no doubt He was "watching over His Word to fulfill it" (Jeremiah 1:12).

One night not long ago my heart was breaking as I sat with Jasmine, seeing her struggle in the darkness of depression yet again. As she opened up to me I asked her, "If you could describe exactly how you are feeling right now, what words would you use?" She said, "Mom, I feel like I'm emotionally drowning." I picked up my notebook where I had written out scriptural prayers for my family, found the first prayer that had her name in it, and started to pray out loud for my daughter. I began to read, "God has redeemed Jasmine. He's called her by name. She's His. When she's in over her head, God is right there with her. When she's in rough waters, she will not go down. When she's between a rock and a hard place, it won't be a dead end. Because you are God, her personal God... You paid a huge price for her. That's how much she means to You. That's how much You love her!" (based on Isaiah 43:1-4).

As I finished the prayer, Jasmine looked at me in amazement and said, "Do you realize what you just read? God just promised me that when I'm in rough waters, I won't drown!" It was a promise for both of us. A promise to Jasmine, that even though she feels like she's drowning, God is there to hold her up. A promise to me, as her mom, that He heard His Word that I prayed back to Him, and that His "Word will never return to Him void" (Isaiah 55:11). Did you catch that? *God heard His Word when it was prayed back to Him.* It's like reminding Him of His own promises to us that are found in His Word. It's moments like that where I am encouraged and reminded that those of us who are on the path to walk by faith and not by sight must learn to believe His Word over what we see and how we feel.

Practicing the Word

God has opened the door for me to share my heart and story with you. I pray that you will be inspired, but more than that, I pray that you will be motivated to not be your own bully. Use this book as a "new beginning" in your journey with God. Pick up your journal/notebook, go to *Biblegateway.com* and find a verse to write out for yourself or someone who needs your prayers. Refer back to my prayers for Jasmine if you need an example.

CHAPTER 3

"I Have Something to Say"

Psalm 27 (AMPC)

4 One thing have I asked of the Lord, that will I seek, inquire
for, and [insistently] require: that I may dwell in the house
of the Lord [in His presence] all the days of my life, to
behold and gaze upon the beauty [the sweet attractiveness
and the delightful loveliness] of the Lord and to meditate,
consider, and inquire in His temple.

8 You have said, Seek My face [inquire for and require My
presence as your vital need]. My heart says to You, Your
face (Your presence), Lord, will I seek, inquire for, and
require [of necessity and on the authority of Your Word].

14 Wait and hope for and expect the Lord; be brave and of
good courage and let your heart be stout and enduring.
Yes, wait for and hope for and expect the Lord.

RECENTLY, I GOT together with two of my close friends,
Summer and Paulette. It had been a while since we had seen
each other, but we have the kind of friendship where we can "pick
up right where we left off." Our first order of business is always to go
around the table and take turns sharing what's been going on in our
lives. The response is always laughing together, crying together, or
applauding each other's accomplishments. During this particular "hang
out session," Summer said something in response to what was shared
that struck a chord with me. She said, "Well, it's different because
now you have something to say." That made me step away from the
conversation for a moment as God reiterated her comment in my spirit,

"Yes, Debbie, I'm calling you to write this book because you have something to say."

You see, I've always had some type of connection with God since I was very young. I believed in Him, sought to know Him, and tried to be the best I could for Him. Interestingly, however, it wasn't until I had some times of total frustration with Him and open rebellion against Him that I started to experience the amazing ways He will reach out to me.

As He called me back into His will for my life, I began to pursue Him on a new level. He connected me with some amazing Christian girlfriends and together we have been pursuing His heart.

The story I feel impressed to share with you in this chapter is one that was hard to go through, but I wouldn't change what it taught me for anything.

I had recently connected with a new church and was on fire for God, along with my newfound friends, whom I met with each week for prayer meeting. God was teaching us new levels of praying and reaching out to Him in faith. We were reading great books on prayer and praying with inspired boldness with those who came to our prayer meetings every week.

One Saturday after church, I decided to take my two young daughters with me to a nursing home to minister with a group from our church. Afterward, some friends of mine, Jim and his wife, Jackie, invited us over to see their home and his music shop. In my mind I was planning to decline since I knew that my daughters were tired and anxious to get home, but I found myself saying, "Sure, we can come over." .

When we got to their home they saw that some of their friends had arrived and were waiting outside. Jim took me and one of my daughters to his music shop to show us where he worked while the rest of the group went with his wife into their home. We had only been in his shop for a few minutes when someone came running from their house yelling, "Come quick! Your wife just fell down and she can't get up!"

We ran to their house and found her lying on the floor having a seizure. Jim proceeded to perform CPR on her while his friend called

911. I stood in the next room with the rest of the group feeling helpless, when the thought came to me, "I brought you here to pray." I gathered everyone in a circle and began to pray out loud. I mustered up every ounce of faith I had and prayed, knowing that God had me there for a purpose, so He would surely hear my prayer and heal Jackie.

They rushed her to the hospital and later that night I received the call that she had died from a brain aneurism.

Wow! That was such a blow to my rising faith! For the next three days I found myself struggling in what I would describe as a "cloud of darkness." So many accusatory thoughts kept plaguing me with messages like, "You really failed. Not only did you fail your friend, you failed God." I struggled to understand what had just happened and why. After three days Cheryl, a friend of mine from church, called me. She said, "Debbie, I just spoke with Jim and you need to know how much you helped him in his time of crisis. He said that because he was engrossed in trying to resuscitate his wife he really couldn't focus on praying. He could hear you praying from the next room and that gave him the courage to face the fact that his wife died, knowing that someone had prayed on her behalf."

As she shared that, the dark cloud lifted from me as I learned in that moment the sovereignty of God. I realized that we are not called to pray so that God can answer in *our* ways, but to invite *His* purpose to be done.

But God wasn't finished teaching me through this story yet.

About a year and a half later I was at prayer meeting and someone I had never met before walked in. She was a young lady and during the course of our meeting she opened up and began to share something that brought me to my knees in humility before God.

She related that she had gone to school with Jackie's daughter a couple of years back. (I can't even type this story now without stopping and worshipping God for all of His greatness!) She began to share how one time when Jackie was visiting their school they all stood in a circle together to pray. As Jackie prayed she asked God for something very specific. She prayed that when it was her time to die that God would bring someone into that moment to be there for her husband.

My heart began to race as my thoughts ran over each other. "What? What did she just say?!!! Are you serious, God? You sent me there that evening not to pray for her to be healed, but to fulfill Jackie's own request that she prayed years ago?" I don't think I've ever been so humbled in all my life! The proportion of how big God really is standing next to tiny little me was magnified about a zillion times in that moment!

I began to think back to the times I went to Jim's house with my friend Carleen and her daughter Amy to help him clean out their house so he wouldn't have to take on that task by himself. In answer to the prayers of Jim's wife, God had called us to be a support for him during the first few months of his grief.

So, here's what I have to say. Here's my voice through experience. God is God. At any given moment He hears every prayer prayed. He sees people's end from their beginning. His thoughts are greater. His ways are higher. He is love. Even though that's just tipping the edge of the eternal iceberg, it's still enough to believe that He hears us when we pray and He knows what He is doing.

Practicing the Word

One of the reasons that it's so important to pray Scripture is that as we discover *who* God is in His Word, it grows our faith to believe that He listens to our prayers and works out the best answer possible for us. Write down the following Scripture as a prayer. Take time to read and pray it for the next week. It will grow your faith for the next time you are in a situation that tempts you to doubt God.

"Lord, how rich are the depths of Your mystery, how deep is Your wisdom and knowledge. I can't possibly trace Your motives for I don't understand all that You do. Who could ever know Your mind? Who could ever try to tell You what to do? Who could ever give You anything? No one, for You are the supreme God. All that exists comes from You, and is for You. To You be glory forever" Romans 11: 33–36 (Prayer Bible).

CHAPTER 4

"Thinking God's Thoughts With Him"

Psalm 27 (CEB)
4 I have asked one thing from the Lord—
    it's all I seek:
    to live in the Lord's house all the days of my life,
    seeing the Lord's beauty
    and constantly adoring his temple.
8 Come, my heart says, seek God's face.
    Lord, I do seek your face!
    Don't leave me all alone!
14 Hope in the Lord!
    Be strong! Let your heart take courage!
    Hope in the Lord!

ONE NIGHT WHEN my younger daughter, Camilia, was about 4 years old, I remember lying down next to her in her bed. It was dark and quiet so I thought that she had finally fallen asleep. Suddenly her little voice broke the silence as she proclaimed with confidence, "Everybody loves me soooo much!" Chuckling, I realized that instead of drifting off to sleep in the silence of the night, she was meditating on certain moments of her life and growing in excitement as she realized how much she was loved!

What we think or meditate on throughout the course of our lives is crucial to what we believe about ourselves and about God. In Psalm 119: 54–55 David shares something beautiful. He writes: "I can't help singing about Your words; they are my theme song wherever I live. In the night I mediate on Your name, O Lord, because it helps me keep Your commands" (Prayer Bible, A Modern Translation). "For as [a man] thinketh in his heart, so is he." Proverbs 23:7a (KJV)

David had a strong relationship with God through meditating on and singing His Word. He understood that the way to plant the Word of God in our hearts is through time spent with it. I can tell you from my personal experience that the most intimate times I've had with God are the moments that I sit, open up His Word, and ask the Holy Spirit to bring the light of God's Word into my heart. As I invite the presence of the Holy Spirit into my time with God's Word, a deep place within my heart opens up. Sometimes I feel a peaceful warmth as I read about the love of God. Other times, there's an overwhelming excitement as God reveals Himself to me in a way that I can barely take in and respond to. I'm left with a greater hunger to get heart to heart with God through His Word.

In Proverbs 4:20–22 King Solomon, the wisest man who ever lived, said, "Let God's Word penetrate deep into your hearts" (NLT), and in Colossians 3:16 Paul wrote, "Let the Word of Christ dwell in you richly."

These amazing men of God knew that there is more to the Bible than just physically having it or even reading it. It needs to *become* part of who we are. With the help of the Holy Spirit, the Word of God comes to life in us as we read, pray, and meditate our way through it.

Wikipedia defines Christian meditation as follows: "Christian meditation is the process of deliberately focusing on specific thoughts (such as a Bible passage) and reflecting on their meaning in the context of the love of God." (Wikipedia "Christian Meditation" - An introduction to Christian spirituality by F. Antonisamy). I love how The Prayer Bible interprets meditation prayer. It describes it as "Thinking God's thoughts with Him. This is thinking about God in His presence" (p 1869).

Let me invite you into an intimate place where I meet with God. Over the years there have been Scriptures that have spoken to me directly from the heart of God. This is the true purpose of Scripture; direct communication to us from the heart of God. I would like to share with you one of those biblical treasures.

The following Scripture is so beautiful because it allows us to glimpse and be part of the amazing relationship that Jesus has with His Father. It's found in John 17. This is one of Jesus' last recorded prayers before He was betrayed, tried, and crucified. Whenever I read this chapter I feel like a veil between Heaven and earth is lifted, and for a brief moment I get a glimpse of the incredible love of God.

Here are my favorite parts of this chapter:

"Father, My hour is come. Glorify Thy Son so I can glorify You... I have glorified You on earth and accomplished the work You sent Me to do. Father, glorify Me with the glory I had in Heaven which I had with You before the world was created. I have given Your Name to the men You gave me... They have received Your Word and they believe it, and they believe I came from Heaven to do Your will... I pray, Holy Father that You would keep them safe, that they may be one, as We are One... Now I come to You, Father, that they may have joy... Make them holy by Your Word, because Your Word is truth... I am not praying for these disciples only, I'm also praying for those who will believe because of their word. I pray that all believers may be one as You and I are One. And the glory You gave Me I give them so they may also be one as We are. I am in them, as You are in Me" (Prayer Bible).

Can't you just imagine it? Jesus is getting ready to face His darkest hour. The destiny of man is in His hands. Knowing that soon He will be arrested, He spends His last night in His prayer garden retreat and He prays for His disciples — for you and for me. What is His prayer? What was the reason that He came down here from Heaven? It was to restore what was lost; the beautiful, intimate relationship between God and His creation. His prayer was for us to be restored to that love.

Let me share with you how I love to pray and meditate on those verses in John 17.

"Jesus, I have received Your Word in my heart. I believe that You came from Heaven to do Your Father's will. Keep me safe, Jesus, so I can be one with You, even as You are One with God. I receive Your joy. I praise You because You are making me holy by Your Word, because Your Word is truth. Thank You for making me one just as You and Your Father are One."

A lot of people don't really know how to relate to the Bible. It can seem mundane, especially if you were raised in church and have "heard it all before." Without the light of the Holy Spirit, the Bible seems like another book full of words. However, as we journey together through this book we will unpack more of what it means to utilize the gift of the Holy Spirit as we spend time in God's Word.

Follow the example of a 4-year-old girl. The more time you spend in the Word reading and thinking about how much God loves you, the more you will feel loved!

Practicing the Word

We don't have to "take on" large portions of Scripture when we meditate. It can be powerful (and easier to remember) to have just one sentence from Scripture that we pray throughout the day. Take one of the thoughts from John 17 below (or find your own) and keep it in front of you, being intentional about saying it several times a day for at least a week.

Jesus, I am receiving Your Word in my heart.

Father, I praise You for making me holy by Your Word, because Your Word is truth.

Jesus, thank You for making me one with You and the Father. Jesus, I receive Your joy.

CHAPTER 5

"When Your Words Remain in Me"

Psalm 27 (CEB)
4 I have asked one thing from the Lord—
   it's all I seek:
   to live in the Lord's house all the days of my life,
   seeing the Lord's beauty
   and constantly adoring his temple.
8 Come, my heart says, seek God's face.
   Lord, I do seek your face!
14 Hope in the Lord!
   Be strong! Let your heart take courage!
   Hope in the Lord!

THE BIBLE IS full of amazing promises. The things that God lays out for us in His Word are full of His love and power. It's one thing to read these promises. It's another step to believe them. The moment of truth comes when we are actually living them.

As I write this chapter I am reading about the life of Jesus in a powerful book called "Messiah" by Jerry D. Thomas. In it the author writes about Jesus: "As He began to understand the society around Him, He saw that its demands were in direct conflict with the teachings of God. Most people had lost sight of God's Word and were following traditions that meant nothing. The services that were supposed to help them understand God brought them no help, no peace. They did not know the freedom of truly serving God" (p. 55).

The more time I spend with God in His Word, the more the eyes of my heart are opened. The Holy Spirit is transforming the words on its pages into the Breath of Life that it's promised to be.

John 15:7 is the first clue to this amazing life we're promised. "Jesus, when I remain settled in You, and Your Words remain in me, I can ask what I want and You'll give it to me." My whole life as a Christian I've heard the last part of this verse preached and prayed on, but I have never actually seen anyone (including myself) step forward and *live* the promise that whatever they want will be given to them. If we back it up a bit to the first part of this verse, I believe that our journey toward truth begins; when I remain in Jesus and His Words remain in me. Okay, now we are on to something! I get excited when I see verses like that (which happen to be all throughout the Bible).

How is God's power to be released through our lives? By Him living in us through His Word. To illustrate my point further, I want to step into the shoes of some of the Bible's greatest heroes. What was it that made them so great, anyway?

The book of Joshua gets me motivated to do miraculous things for God! The very first chapter of this book is packed with an amazing promise! "As I promised Moses, so I promise you that the land will be yours wherever you go... I will be with you as I was with Moses and no one will be able to defeat you. I will never leave you alone or abandon you. Be strong and brave as you lead My people... I repeat, be strong and brave. And obey all the laws Moses gave you. If you follow them carefully, you will succeed wherever you are. Your success depends on your studying them, thinking about them all the time, and obeying them. As I've said, be strong and brave. Don't be afraid or discouraged, just remember I will be right there with you wherever you go" (Prayer Bible).

Something deep, powerful, and holy gets stirred in me when I read this chapter. Just think about it. Joshua is getting ready to fill the shoes of one of the all-time greatest men of God. He has to not only face and lead a multitude of stubborn people, but also face his fears. God steps in to speak to and encourage Joshua (which He will always do when we face our fears and follow His lead). Of all the things God could have said, of all the ways to embolden and empower Joshua, He comes up with one piece of advice — one secret to his success; one thing that will make or break this Moses-shoes-filling-man. God commands, "Study and think about My Word all the time!" Are you getting excited yet? I mean, really, that's the secret? That's the ticket to victory and success? Absolutely! And if you're still not convinced, let's move on to our next hero.

I mentioned earlier in this book that Psalm 119 beautifully unpacks David's relationship with God through His Word. God Himself calls David a "man after My own heart." That's how I want God to describe me, so tapping into David's secret is a part of my journey, and I pray that it will become a part of yours, too.

"Bless me so I may live before You and keep the Word You have given. Open my eyes so I can see wonderful truths in Your law" (17–18).

"Renew my life with Your Words. Fulfill Your Scriptures to me so that I may worship You in awe" (37–38).

"Remember the Word You have given to me because I have put my trust in it. I take comfort in what You have said because Your Word gives me hope" (49–50).

"O Lord, I love Your law; I meditate on it all day long" (97).

"I lay awake through the different hours of the night meditating on the promises of Your Word" (149).

"I rejoice in Your Scripture like someone finding great treasure" (162).

"They who love Your Scriptures will have great peace and nothing shall offend them" (165).

That intimate place that David found with God; the place that kept him strong during the years he had to run for his life, continuing to believe that he was called to be king; that place was knowing God through His Word. Through thinking about, meditating on, and singing God's heart through His Words, David experienced the reality that the Word is full of life and power (Hebrews 4:12).

I've tapped into that place. I have so much more treasure to find, so many more moments ahead of me that I can't wait to experience with God. I would compare it to the growth of a tree. The reason it is able to grow strong, reaching higher and higher toward the sun is because below the surface, where it's dark and no one can see, there are roots growing deeper, longer, and stronger that feed the tree and support its strength.

Every time I sit with God, my Bible in hand, I'm getting deeper roots. I've come to see my time with God as being so precious and invaluable. I read. A lot. I've read many great books by incredible authors who have inspired me and shown me through their own experiences that nothing is impossible for God. I put down their books with renewed determination to be able to say with my dying breath what Jesus said, "God, I've accomplished all that You put me on this planet to do" (John 17:4, paraphrased).

However, when I open my Bible it's different. I'm not just reading about the hearts of God's people, I'm tapping into the very heart of God. I read about His love, His promises, His frustrations with mankind, and His grace. The Holy Spirit, the same One who spoke the breath of God into the men as they wrote the Bible, speaks to me as I read it. That's one of the reasons He was sent here, and I'm so grateful.

Moving forward in the Bible we meet up with Paul. The New Testament is full of beautiful prayers that Paul wrote and sent out to the churches to encourage them as they faced persecution, death, and worldly distractions on a daily basis. Let's listen in on one of his prayers found in Colossians 3:12. "Since you are all set apart by God, made holy and dearly loved, clothe yourselves with a holy way of life: compassion, kindness, humility, gentleness, and patience... Forgive... But above all these, put on love... Let the word of the Anointed One richly inhabit your lives." (The Voice).

As I read this, what really jumps out at me is the last line, "Let the word of the Anointed One richly inhabit your lives" From my study and experience, it is the key to the rest of the chapter. If we want to live holy lives as laid out here by Paul, the Word of God must inhabit us. God's people weren't the only ones who recognized and lived by this secret. Even Jesus lived the power of God through His Word.

In the book I referred to earlier, "Messiah," the author refers to how Jesus lived out the Word of God. "Jesus had a simple reply: 'Show

Me where it says so in the Scriptures.' He would listen to anything from God's Word, but He wasn't interested in human inventions. Jesus seemed to know the Scriptures from beginning to end."

Jesus' empowerment from His Father, through His Word, is demonstrated in Matthew 4. As we enter this story, take a moment with me to think back to a time before the creation of man. We step into this story when the angel who led the worship team in Heaven rebelled and was cast from the presence of God. From the first moment that he heard of the Son of God's commitment to save mankind, to the moment of Jesus' birth, and all the way to Matthew 4 when Jesus was faced with the devil himself, the fallen angel had been using all of his powers to devise a scheme to bring down this Savior. This was no joke. He had been scheming in the darkest hours of the night for centuries to come up with the perfect plan, the ultimate temptations that he was convinced could not be overcome. In "Messiah" Jerry D. Thomas writes, "Satan saw that he must either destroy Jesus or be destroyed. He would fight this battle personally, and all the weapons of Hell would be used." Wow. This is the ultimate battle between good and evil. Our destiny was dangling by a thread in the hands of our enemy and in the face of Jesus. Just how would Jesus stay strong enough in this battle?

The answer opens up a deeper place in my heart and spirit. A place of longing for more of what Jesus had in this story. Herein lies His secret...

"It is written..."

Jesus knew the Scriptures, but knowing is not enough. Even Satan knows Scripture. If God's Word were only in Jesus' mind, He would not have been able to defeat Satan. But God's Word was also in His heart and in His spirit. Every early morning excursion that He took to a garden or mountaintop He connected with His Father through prayer and through His Word. How do we know this? If you go to verse 4 of Matthew chapter 4 Jesus answered His first temptation with these words, "Man shall not live by bread alone, but by every word that comes from the mouth of God." I don't think it's a coincidence here that the Word is compared with bread. Bread doesn't do us any good if we don't eat it. We can buy it, bring it home, and put it in our kitchen cupboard, but if we never take the time to get it out and actually eat it, there's no hope of it filling our stomachs or strengthening our bodies.

Jesus ingested the Word every day. It's amazing to think that He, being fully God yet fully human, had to take the time to know God through His Word. How much more should we, who are born human and spend our lives battling our flesh, be in the Word of God regularly. God will begin to plant it deep within us and soon it will reap a harvest called "relationship" with Him.

Practicing the Word

Think of a temptation that you face. It could be a crossroad choosing between what you know is right and what you know is wrong. It could be a temptation to respond to people in anger or jealousy. Maybe pride is a challenge you face. Whatever it is, I am encouraging you to take time right now to visit *Biblegateway.com*. Plug in a key word such as "anger" or "forgiveness" or "love." Write down one or two Scriptures as prayers to keep with you. Practice saying them so that the next time your "temptation" shows up you can fight back with your "It is written" Scripture.

Example: Colossians 3:13–14, The Message (MSG)

"So, chosen by God for this new life of love, dress in the wardrobe God picked out for you: compassion, kindness, humility, quiet strength, discipline. Be even-tempered...quick to forgive an offense... And regardless of what else you put on, wear love."

Prayer: God, because You have chosen me, I have the power to be a person of compassion, kindness, and humility. Thank You for giving me the ability to forgive and to love others as You do. In Jesus' name, Amen.

CHAPTER 6

"When God Responds"

Psalm 27 (ERV)
4 I ask only one thing from the Lord.
   This is what I want most:
   Let me live in the Lord's house all my life,
   enjoying the Lord's beauty
   and spending time in his palace.[a]
8 My heart told me to come to you, Lord,
   so I am coming to ask for your help.
14 Wait for the Lord's help.
   Be strong and brave,
   and wait for the Lord's help.

IT WAS ONE of those times when God must have just looked down and smiled. I'd been seeking God with my whole heart, knowing the Scriptures with familiarity, that if we seek Him, we will find Him (Proverbs 8:17; Jeremiah 29:13). I was meeting with Michelle, a spiritually-inspiring friend who was sharing her story with me of how God was leading her to set up a ministry office in her home. That struck a chord with me and I was reminded, or rather prompted by the Holy Spirit, that I needed to convert a room in our home into an office space to use for ministry. I'd had that prompting several times over the last few years, but felt that the time was "now."

When I mentioned it to Michelle, who is also an amazing interior decorator, she offered to help me decorate the space. So here we go, two women who love the Lord and love to shop, feeling inspired to make this happen! She did an incredible job of making my new office a beautiful place of inspiration! It was perfect, except for one thing. I didn't have a desk to use or a chair to sit in. I really wanted God to be a part of this whole process since this is the space where I would meet regularly with Him. As I looked at my beautifully decorated office and my eyes scanned over the empty space where my desk would go, I felt an inner voice say, "Ask me to provide a desk for you." Now here's an interesting place to find ourselves. We can ask God over and over to speak to us, and when He does with that still small voice, we may excuse it as something else and decide to not listen. I'm learning to listen. So, in that same deep place of my heart where I felt the voice I responded, "Okay, God. Please provide me with a desk."

Less than two days later I was out with Lael, another great friend whose life inspires me, celebrating her recent retirement. In the process of chatting and catching up I mentioned how Michelle had helped me decorate a new office space. Lael interrupted me in mid sentence and asked, "Do you have a desk?" I replied, "No. Not yet." To which she quickly responded, "I have one I've been wanting to give away. Do you want to go look at it this afternoon?" I couldn't believe how quickly God answered the prayer He prompted me to pray! Not only did she give me a desk that is the perfect style and size for the space I had, but she gave me a matching chair to go with it. She also told me that she'd been wanting to give it away for a long time, but "something" kept her from doing it!

Here's the bottom line — it's not about the desk. It's completely about God. Through this, and so many other stories, He's teaching me the necessity of listening to His voice, obeying, and then trusting Him for the outcome.

So, here I am with this amazing office, feeling blessed by two special friends and an incredible God. What I didn't know was that God had not yet put the icing on His cake. That same week I got a surprise package in the mail. It was from David, an incredibly talented guy who has been one of my best friends since the fifth grade. I opened it and to my surprise I found a metal statue of a woman kneeling in prayer, and engraved at the bottom was, "I prayed to the Lord, and He answered me. He freed me from all my fears" Psalm 34:4. In the box was a note that said, "I love that you are following your calling and pouring your heart into it. This is for your ministry room." Receiving that unexpected gift filled my heart with complete joy and gratitude!

When God responds to hearts that seek Him through prayer and through His Word, He shows up in unexpected and exciting ways. The Bible is full of promises because He is a God Who loves to bless us. (See Psalm 37:3-7; Jeremiah 17:7-8; Isaiah 51:3-4) There are two reasons why it is imperative that we spend time in His Word. First, knowing how to pray is based on knowing Who we are praying to. God's heart and character are portrayed beautifully in the Bible. Second, God responds to faith, and we can't have faith in the Word or in God if we don't spend the time needed with Him. We must agree that He is Who He says He is and that He does what He says He will do.

Practicing the Word

Some of us may pick up the Bible with certain mindsets or doubts. I urge you to pick it up regardless of how you are "feeling." With anything that promises a great reward we have to invest time and patience. I am telling you from personal experience that this will give you a greater reward then anything else you could invest your time and faith into.

I am reading a book called "Witness to Fitness" by Donna Richardson Joyner. In her book she encourages her readers to write up what she calls "W2Fit cards." She states, "I list my goals on the cards, decorate them, and at the bottom of each I write, 'It's Possible.' I post my W2Fit cards on my mirror in my bathroom, carry them in my purse or briefcase, and keep them on my desk, so I can always have with me my vision of what I will accomplish. W2Fit cards are daily reminders of me being a witness to my faith, family, purpose, and passion."

I've done the same thing with Scriptures. Our lives are so busy that if we aren't intentional about focusing on God's Word throughout the day we won't get very far. I've even kept some Scripture cards in my car with the intention of reading them while waiting at red lights. There are so many traffic lights in our area that I thought this would give me a lot of time in the Word. Do you know that once I made that decision I hit every light green? That never happens in the Washington, D.C. area!

You can also do something innovative with your phone or computer. There are so many apps out there that can facilitate keeping God's Word in front of us. If you type a scriptural reference in Google (ex: Psalm 119:43) and then click on "images" it gives you beautiful pictures with the text written on them. If you make one your screen saver you will see it every time you pick up your device. Each time you see it, take a moment to read it as a prayer. After a couple of weeks replace it with a new Scripture photo.

CHAPTER 7

"The Process"

Psalm 27 (EXB)
4 I ask only one thing from the Lord.
  This is what I ·want [seek after]:
  Let me ·live [dwell] in the Lord's house [the sanctuary]
  all the days of my life.
  Let me see the Lord's beauty
  and ·look with my own eyes [make inquiry; discover God's
  will] at his Temple.
8 My heart said of you, "Go, ·worship him [seek his face]."
  So I ·come to worship you [seek your face], Lord.
14 Wait for [Hope in] the Lord's help.
  Be strong and let your heart be brave,
  and ·wait for [hope in] the Lord's help.

HAVE YOU EVER felt speechless? That's me, right now, sitting in this chair, trying to figure out how to express to you in words who God is to me.

The Bible tells us to earnestly remember the things that God has done in our lives (1 Chronicles 16). That's why I journal, make scrapbook pages of things I read that I want to keep in front of me, and why I have a vision board in my ministry office (thanks to my ministry room decorator, Michelle) But, as I look back at how amazing God has been to me and the incredible ways He continues to show up in my life, I'm so overwhelmed by it all that I have no words to describe it.

In spite of that, I'm not discouraged. Am I a writer? No. Did I excel in English class when I was a student? No. I only took the English classes in college that were required of me. I did well in those classes, but no one ever told me that I was great at it or that I had a gift and should go into writing.

The reason I share this is because this is one of the times that I tap into the power of God's Word. I believe that God has called me to write this book, and once again I find myself facing the fear of the unknown. Looking back I realize that God has never once called me to do anything that I had a degree in or experience with. I'd like to take a moment now to thank Him for that because, without those times of having to face fear, I never would have discovered where to find faith.

I have a worn red notebook that I journaled my way through several years ago. In it I've copied powerful Scriptures of who God says I am and what He's called me to do. In addition, I've written out quotes from books by my spiritual mentors, such as Joyce Meyer, T. D. Jakes, and Beth Moore. Anytime I begin to feel overwhelmed or fearful because God is calling me yet again out of my comfort zone, I will sit down, take out that notebook, and begin to read out loud what is written there.

Just today I was reading "Live Love Lead" by Brian Houston, the founder of Hillsong Church in Australia. In it he writes, "Who does God say you are, and what has he called you to do? The key to living a life of purpose is being able to answer these questions" (p.38). The reason I have made it this far in my God vision is because He answers these questions for me when I spend time with Him in His Word. If I didn't have the gift of the Word I would feel lost, groping in the dark, trying to figure out on my own what my life's purpose is. It would be an overwhelming task.

I have other journals where I've recorded amazing things that God has done in my life, and I go back and read those stories as another way of strengthening my belief that God is with me in my journey.

Things began getting really exciting for me when I started to do that and I saw how God responded. It gets so crazy sometimes that my only response can be worship! There have been times when I'll find a Scripture and realizing how perfectly it fits my need, I'll pray it over myself.

I have invested a lot of time praying Scripture over myself to prepare my heart to minister to people. There have been many times when I've had to face fears head on with His Word. One of the areas I feel ill-equipped to serve in is singing on a praise [music] team at my church. I can't begin to count the number of thoughts of doubt and defeat that the devil has thrown at me since I decided to become part of a worship team several years ago.

God led me to dig my heels in and cast down those thoughts with the power in His words. These are some of my favorites:

> "The reverent fear and worship of the Lord is my treasure and His" (Isaiah 33:6).
>
> "And He put a new song in my mouth, a song of praise to our God. Many shall see and fear and put their trust and confident reliance in the Lord" (Psalm 40:3).
>
> "I ascribe to the Lord glory and strength. I give to the Lord glory and strength. I give to the Lord the glory due His name; I worship the Lord in the beauty of holiness... the voice of the Lord is powerful; the voice of the Lord is full of majesty... The Lord sits as King forever! The Lord will give (unyielding and impenetrable) strength to me; the Lord will bless me with peace" (Psalm 29).

I faithfully meditated on these Scriptures as I prayed them over my life and was continually amazed with how God fulfilled His Word in my life and ministry. I remember once when I was leading worship and a middle school-aged boy approached me after the service was finished. He was visiting from another state with his class and came up to me to ask for my autograph. I was so shocked that I almost laughed at his request. As I gave him my autograph my heart filled with joy and gratitude as I recognized God's hand of encouragement behind it. Numerous times I've had people approach me to thank me for how much I minister to them spiritually when I'm up front singing, speaking, or praying. They have no idea of the battle that's waging in my mind as I set my heart to worship God no matter how I feel.

One time when I was under a major spiritual attack I had to step forward in faith to worship God on our team. That afternoon I got a phone call from someone who was at the service. He called to ask me about the new song we had sung. He said it was so powerful that he had to find it and listen to it again. Then he said to me, "The way you lead worship is so inspiring. You need to be up there leading worship every week!" I can't adequately describe what that declaration meant to me. I was in a place of great emotional pain, determined not to give up, and I knew that his call was God's way of rewarding my worship that morning in spite of my circumstances.

I was leading my women's group at church recently and I was sharing the importance of facing our fears of inadequacy. As I shared my insecurity with singing on my praise team, Michelle, one of the women in the group, spoke up saying, "I can't believe that you feel that way. I have to share a story with you. Several years ago I was able to convince my dad to visit church with us. He had left the church years ago and had no interest in getting reconnected. That particular day you were on the praise team. As he saw you worship he recognized the presence of God on your life so powerfully that that became one of the things that eventually brought him back to attending church."

I share these things with you as my testimony that God is incredibly and consistently faithful. I pray that my stories (and there are so many more I could share) reveal to you how God fulfills His call on our lives through the Scriptures we speak over ourselves. He intimately watches over us and lifts us up by the power of His Word because He knows how hard life can get sometimes.

Practicing the Word

As you continue your time in God's Word you will find Scriptures that will grab your attention and stir a desire to embrace them in your life. When that happens write them out with *your* name in them as a confession of what God is doing in your life.

Here's an example:

"If anyone speaks, they should do so as one who speaks the very words of God. If anyone serves, they should do so with the strength God provides, so that in all things God may be praised through Jesus Christ" (1 Peter 4:11 NIV).

Italics added to illustrate how Scripture can be written in the first person tense.

As *I* speak, *I* speak the very Words of God. As *I* serve, *I* do it with the strength that God provides so that *my* life will praise God through Jesus Christ.

CHAPTER 8

"Oneness"

Psalm 27 (GW)
4 I have asked one thing from the Lord.
  This I will seek:
  to remain in the Lord's house all the days of my life
  in order to gaze at the Lord's beauty
  and to search for an answer in his temple.
8 When you said,
  "Seek my face,"
  my heart said to you,
  "O Lord, I will seek your face."
14 Wait with hope for the Lord.
  Be strong, and let your heart be courageous.
  Yes, wait with hope for the Lord.

I MENTIONED EARLIER in this book that I love John 15 and 16 because these chapters invite us to live intimately with God. God loves intimacy. With us. Every day.

I'm feeling particularly blessed right now. God knows how crazy my life is, running in so many directions at one time. He also knows that in order for me to write this book I needed to be separated from all my distractions. So He sent me all the way to Australia to be with Him. My husband, Chris, is here on a business trip. But I feel that God brought me here just to be with Him. That's what this time is all about. Yes, I'm writing this book, and I believe that He has a divine purpose for it, but my time here (He's given me a whole month!) is centered on days of getting heart-to-heart with Him.

You see, this is not just a book about my ideas and experiences; it is my encounter with the One, true, living God. In Acts 4 the Bible says something that I want to incorporate into my everyday life. It says that as the people saw the disciples they "took note that they had been with Jesus."

I've read books like that before. Books where an author's anointing came alive as I read the words they had written. Words are powerful. They are God's avenues into the hearts of man.

Every day as I wake up here in Australia and realize that I have another day to focus on nothing else but God, I am in awe that He would orchestrate so many details of my life so that I can have uninterrupted time with Him. I spend hours each day reading the Word and inspirational books from anointed authors (such as Holley Gerth, Mark Batterson, and Lloyd John Ogilvie), journaling, and then writing what He puts on my heart.

You may be thinking, "I wish He did that for me." Well, He did! This book is for you. He wants more than anything to take His relationship with you to the next level. He wants you to hear His voice and His heart through His Word. I am not only praying, but also declaring with boldness that this book will create in people's hearts a growing desire to know God through His Word. It is an amazing journey, and as we continue our time together in this book, I hope that you will take advantage of the "Practicing the Word" sections at the end of each chapter.

I pray that with every word that's read from this book you will see and take note that I have been with Jesus.

Practicing the Word

We can spend our lives wishing that we knew Jesus and could hear from Him or we can invest time in His presence, believing that we will be rewarded. Take a moment now to write down the things that monopolize your time. Ask God to show you what changes you must make so that you can have designated time to seek Him each day. If that seems too overwhelming for you at this time then find a way to include him in the busyness. For example, you can buy a dramatized audio version of the Bible online or on CD and listen to it during your daily morning commute.

CHAPTER 9

"When It Hurts"

Psalm 27 (GNT)
4 I have asked the Lord for one thing;
  one thing only do I want:
  to live in the Lord's house all my life,
  to marvel there at his goodness,
  and to ask for his guidance.
8 When you said, "Come worship me,"
  I answered, "I will come, Lord."
14 Trust in the Lord.
  Have faith, do not despair.
  Trust in the Lord.

THIS MORNING AS I sat with God I felt impressed to share the story of my father's death. It's been almost eight years since we lost him.

He was only 63, still working full time, and had recently had a heart valve replaced. The doctor told him that it was a simple surgery and he would feel a lot more energy once he recovered. He was living in Maine with my mom, near my sister and her family and had gotten the doctor's "OK" to come down to Maryland and spend time with me, my brother, and our families.

Just a few days into my parents' vacation, my dad started to feel a lot of pain. We took him to a nearby hospital and after examining him, they transferred him to Johns Hopkins Hospital in Baltimore. Our first thought was, "Thank you, God, that he is here where he can get treated at one of the top hospitals in our country!"

My sister Tammy and her son came down from Maine and she, my mom, and I took turns around the clock, sitting with dad in his hospital room. The doctors determined that my father was dealing with three major infections in the heart valve that had recently been replaced. They said that he was too weak for them to operate, so after a few weeks of rest and treatment their plan was to replace it with a different valve.

During his hospital stay, friends of ours—Eric and Georgina, and Ann, one of our church pastors—came to visit and pray with him. Looking back, I am so grateful to them. My father was a private man in many aspects, one being his walk with God. He was a Christian and went to church regularly, but he never communicated with others what his walk with God was like. It was during those hospital visits and prayer times that I saw my father respond to God in powerful ways. Those moments give me reassurance that I will see him in Heaven.

We knew that his recovery would be long, but we were fully confident in the amazing medical care he was receiving. So I was totally shocked by the phone call I received from my sister just a few days later. She and my mom had been with my father at the hospital that morning and he had taken a turn for the worse. The doctors realized that the infection had gotten so bad that it was breaking through the walls of his heart. The only way to save him was to operate, but his condition was too compromised for him to survive a surgery.

I knew that God could miraculously heal him. I raced to the hospital, my Bible in hand, and surrounded my father's hospital bed, together with Tammy and my sister-in-law, Vickie. We prayed, did we ever pray! We prayed out loud, claiming God's Word, His love, and His power. I thought, "God, You can really show up and show out here! Think of how many people will see Your glory!" We prayed and prayed all the way through to my father's last breath.

I remember it so clearly. Looking down at my father for the first time, knowing that the breath of life had left him. It was a defining moment. A crossroad. God wasted no time in speaking to my heart. The message came through instantly with full impact. He said, "Debbie, you have a choice to make. Are you going to continue to follow Me and believe, or are you going to give in to anger and blame Me for this?"

Somehow I knew that this moment in time would set the stage for my future with God. I've seen since then what can happen to people who don't let God in to heal their grief-stricken hearts. It can change a person and lead them into a pit that is hard to escape from. I knew in that moment that I had to choose God and not entertain even for a second the devil's lies that God had let me down.

The ways that God began to show up for me as I held on to Him were amazing. My sister had been reading a book while she sat by my father in the hospital and since she had finished it, she gave it to me to read. The book is called "Redeeming Love," by Francine Rivers. As I read that book the love of God shone through the story powerfully and right into my grieving heart. At the same time, I was asked to join our choir for a special Christmas event at our church. The music was so healing for me. There were two songs in particular that mirrored the story in the book I was reading and as we practiced and performed them, I could literally see the scenes from the book played out. They were scenes that depicted how God fights for us, loves us, and restores us. Those moments were real and healing for me.

Another avenue of healing for me was a large poster — a beautiful image of an eagle, wings spread, soaring high with a bright, blue sky behind it. Below the image was a Scripture that said, "But those who hope in the Lord will renew their strength. They will soar on wings like eagles; they will run and not grow weary, they will walk and not be faint" (Isaiah 40:31). I put the poster on my refrigerator and every day I looked at that image and verse, praying it into my heart.

Looking back, I realize that I never once asked God what His will was for my father. I stepped out in faith with Scripture ready to back up my prayers that God would answer me my way. I really believe that God used that opportunity to reach my father's heart. This is where we really have to dig our heels in and remember that God loves us, and if we knew everything as He does, we wouldn't ever want anything different than what He chooses.

This story brings me to our next journey in this book: following God's lead. Prayer is important and being in God's Word is essential.

But the other thing that must be a part of the equation is hearing and following the voice of the Holy Spirit.

Practicing the Word

Go online or visit a Christian store such as "Hobby Lobby." Find something that has a powerful Scripture written on it that you can put in your home or office. Every time you see it pray that Scripture into your heart. As you pray, believe that God is changing your life through His Word.

CHAPTER 10

"The Holy Spirit in Prayer"

Psalm 27 (ISV)
4 I have asked one thing from the Lord;
   it is what I really seek:
   that I may remain in the Lord's Temple
   all the days of my life,
   to gaze on the beauty of the Lord;
   and to inquire in his Temple.
8 My mind recalls your word,
   "Seek my face,"
   so your face, Lord, I will seek.
14 Wait on the Lord.
   Be courageous, and he will strengthen your heart.
   Wait on the Lord!

THE HOLY SPIRIT speaks the "deep things of God" (1 Corinthians 2:10). He is the revealer, the corrector, and the comforter. He communicates with us in many ways. As New Year's Eve approached to ring in the beginning of this year, I was contemplating if and what I should commit to as a New Year's resolution. A still, small voice stirred within me, "Use this year to study about Who the Holy Spirit is."

I've been reading some life-changing, truth-empowered books about the Holy Spirit for the past seven months. Together with what I'm learning as laid out in the Bible, they've transformed not only the way I pray, but also the way that I hear from God.

When we read God's Word there are steps we must take to plant His Word in our hearts so that what we read becomes who we are and how we live. Romans 10:17 is one of those steps. "So faith comes from hearing the message, and the message that is heard is what Christ spoke." You can't hear something if it isn't spoken. In Psalm 119:129–131 David writes, "I get understanding when I read Your Word... I open my mouth to receive Your Scriptures."

These past few years of speaking God's Word out loud in prayer have transformed my prayer life. This year, as I'm not only studying about the Holy Spirit, but also desiring to live intimately with God through the Spirit's presence in my life, I take my "steps" by reading/praying Scriptures like this:

"Lord, I thank You for the help of the Holy Spirit who comes to assist me in my weakness. I don't know how I ought to pray, but the Holy Spirit intercedes for me. He prays with words I can't understand or express. What the Holy Spirit prays for me is in agreement with You, my heavenly Father. Therefore the things that will happen to me are for my good because He prays for me" (Romans 8:26–28).

The Bible says that if we pray God's will (praying in Jesus' name) He will hear us, He will respond, and He will answer us (John 14:13–14). That's why I'm writing this book — to share with the world what God has been teaching me and how it's been transforming my life. The only way to know God's will is to spend time with and pray His Word together with the empowering presence of the Holy Spirit.

A great illustration of this is found in the lives of Jesus' disciples. They walked and ministered with Jesus (Who is the Word made flesh — John 1). They saw the power of God daily released through His life as He defeated demons, healed the sick, and even brought the dead back to life. They knew "The Word" more intimately than anyone else during that time. Yet it wasn't until after He returned to Heaven and sent the indwelling power of the Holy Spirit that they had the faith and confidence to release God's will through prayer and perform the same miracles that Jesus had done. The Holy Spirit had transformed them from self-serving, weak-faithed men into men who were so filled by God that they could step into any situation and know His will. They lived with such certainty that when they spoke, the power of Heaven showed up to do the impossible!

DEBBIE HOWELL

There's a place of Christian frustration that I feel I need to address at this point. We live in a time when we often don't know if God will speak to us. We go to church in hopes that something the preacher says, or maybe something that is prayed during the service will address our struggles or strengthen us in our weakness, but to actually believe that the God of the Old Testament or the Jesus of the New Testament will show up for us as in biblical times seems improbable.

I'm about to share something with you that I've shared with very few people. I've been praying about whether I should include it in this book, and I feel impressed that this is the time and place to be vulnerable through my story.

About 10 years ago God was bringing me out of a pit that I had dug for myself. He was forgiving and healing me as I sought Him each morning in the early hours of each day. I knew that through study and prayer I could seek Him, but what I wasn't prepared for was the way He would respond.

I was lying down next to my daughter Camilia one night, waiting for her to fall asleep. As usual, I fell asleep before she did. As I started waking up in the darkness of her room something unusual happened. I was in a half-awake half-asleep state and something very powerful began to play in my mind. It was strange because I wasn't asleep so it wasn't a dream, but it wasn't something that I was intentionally thinking about either. It was almost like a movie had been set on auto-play and was running through my mind on its own. In this scene I saw myself standing in front of my church with my Bible in hand. I was preaching so passionately from the heart of God that I literally had tears in my eyes as I lay in bed watching it. The whole scene lasted for mere seconds, but it left a profound impact on me. For a few days I prayed, asking for understanding as to what had happened and what it meant. After some time passed, I went on with life and didn't give it much more thought. A few weeks later, the exact same thing happened in the same place as I was waking up in my daughter's bed. Once again, I felt that something of significance had happened, but I didn't know what to make of it.

Shortly after that I was up early one morning, spending my time with God, when the Holy Spirit reminded me of my two "dreams." In response I prayed, "God, if you are trying to communicate with me please speak one more time." That same week I was reading a book by Jim Cymbala. In his book he related an experience he had while preaching to a stadium full of men. He shared how the night before he had wrestled with God regarding what he should preach on, because he wasn't comfortable with the topic God chose. In the early hours of the morning he fully gave in to the prompting of the Holy Spirit and when he stepped forward to preach what was on God's heart, he was so powerfully led by the Holy Spirit that it was as if he was watching what was happening instead of being the one sharing the message. In response, thousands of men stepped forward to recommit their lives to God. As I read his story it reminded me of what God had been showing me in those "dreams." I suddenly realized that what I had seen were what I can only understand as visions and God was showing me His plan for my life.

All throughout the Bible God communicates with His people. One of the ways He chooses to speak is through visions. In Habakkuk 2 God reveals how important it is for us not only to listen when He speaks in visions, but also to record and remember them so they can fulfill their purpose in our lives.

"And the Lord answered me: 'Write the vision; make it plain on tablets, so he may run who reads it. For still the vision awaits its appointed time; it hastens to the end – it will not lie. If it seems slow, wait for it; it will surely come; it will not delay'" (Habakkuk 2: 2–3, ESV).

We each have our own learning style. I am a visual learner and since God knows that I believe He also knew that visions would be the best way to help me understand and always remember His message.

I've had a couple of visions since then. They are always quick, powerful, and give me more of an insight into God's plan for my life. During this same time I was listening to a lot of CDs by the Christian music group, Casting Crowns. The messages in those songs powerfully mirrored my journey with God. I listened to the CDs so many times that I knew the songs by heart, and they became prayers that I prayed as I sang.

One day as I was driving in my car I was listening to "The Word is Alive" by Casting Crowns when suddenly I had another five-second vision. As I listened to the lyrics of that song I saw myself standing in front of my church. My Bible was opened in my hands and there was a bright ray of light that came down from Heaven to my Bible and then shot out straight to the people. This was the first time God revealed to me that He was calling me to preach the light of His Word that connects straight to His heart.

You may be able to relate to my story, or the whole thing may seem odd to you. Either way, the point I'm making here is that God still speaks to His people. His Word is a precious gift that He's given that enables us to know Him and His will for our lives. There are other ways that He is fully capable of communicating with us, but you have to know His Word so that you will have the wisdom to discern whether what you are hearing is from Him.

Practicing the Word

Spend some time in prayer thinking about ways you might be holding God in a "box." It's important to approach God with whatever level of faith you have. You may need to pray through wrong thoughts such as:

> "God doesn't speak to His people anymore."
> "God isn't concerned enough to listen to my prayers."
> "If people say they hear from God in a way that I haven't, then it must all be in their heads."
> "God may have communicated with people and done miracles in the Bible, but it's wrong to believe that He will do the same today."

For the next few days practice Psalm 46:10, "Be still, and know that I am God; I will be exalted among the nations, I will be exalted in the earth. The Lord Almighty is with us." Earlier in the chapter David says, "He lifts His voice."

Before you move on to the next chapter take some sticky notes and write on them: "Be still and know that I am God." Put them around your house, in your car, and at work. Whenever you see them, take three seconds to pray that Scripture and practice using your faith as you believe that in the stillness of His presence He will speak to you.

CHAPTER 11

"Faith"

Psalm 27 (TLB)

4 The one thing I want from God, the thing I seek most of all, is the privilege of meditating in his Temple, living in his presence every day of my life, delighting in his incomparable perfections and glory.

8 My heart has heard you say, "Come and talk with me, O my people." And my heart responds, "Lord, I am coming."

14 Don't be impatient. Wait for the Lord, and he will come and save you! Be brave, stouthearted, and courageous. Yes, wait and he will help you.

I'VE LEARNED A lot about faith over the past few years. I've heard that faith is the opposite of fear, that without faith it is impossible to please God (Hebrews 11:6), and that faith means living and believing God's Word more than what we see or how we feel. That's a tough one. We are so driven by our surroundings and locked into our present condition by our feelings. For this reason and so many more, God gave us the truth and power of His Word so that faith could become a reality for us.

One of my "faith-defining moments" came as I listened to a sermon series by televangelist Creflo Dollar. His message unpacked the Bible's imagery of seed, time, and harvest (2 Corinthians 9:10). I realized through his message that when I spend time with God in His Word, reading it, speaking it, and praying it, I am sowing seeds. Just as a farmer has to believe that his planted seeds are growing even before he sees evidence above ground, we need to approach our time in the Word with anticipation of a coming harvest.

The harvest we are believing for is faith. Faith is the fuel that ignites God's Word here on earth. I'm going to revisit a key Scripture to illustrate my point. Romans 10:17 says, "faith comes from hearing, and hearing the Word of God." God Himself has said, "He who comes to me must believe that I exist and that I am a rewarder of those who diligently seek me" (Hebrews 11:6).

Before we see it and even before we feel it, we need to approach our time in God's Word with an anticipation that He will respond.

Here are some powerful texts that will help you begin your faith journey:

> "No Word from God will ever fail." (Luke 1:37)
> "So is My Word that goes out from My mouth. It will not return to me empty, but will accomplish what I desire." (Isaiah 55:11)
> "I am watching to see that My Word is fulfilled." (Jeremiah 1:12)
> "I accept instruction from His mouth and lay up His Words in my heart." (Job 22:22)
> "The Word is very near me; it's in my mouth and in my heart." (Deuteronomy 30:14)
> "The Words I spoke are Spirit and life." (John 6:63)
> "The Word of God is alive and active." (Hebrews 4:12)

I heard something recently that piqued my interest. A preacher was talking about God's Word being compared to a double-edged sword in Hebrews 4:12. His interpretation was that the Word is two-sided because of its relationship with us and with God. One side of its power comes from the fact that God spoke it from Heaven. The other side of the sharp sword is realized when we get in agreement with God by speaking His Word here on earth in faith.

Out of curiosity I asked my husband, Chris, to explain to me the purpose of a double-edged sword. He said that it is more powerful and effective because you can swing it in either direction and it will cut through a line of soldiers in a battle or thick brush in a forest to clear a path.

I love that imagery and here's why. The very first place that we need to experience the power of God's Word is deep within our own hearts. We all have struggles, strongholds, and even addictions that separate us from experiencing the joy and freedom that Jesus died to give us. The double-edged sword in Hebrews promises to "pierce the unseen things such as my soul and spirit, exposing thoughts and attitudes for what they are." The Word of God is meant to clear a path through the "deep jungles of our hearts." God has given us the power to overcome and be set free.

Practicing the Word

Choose two or three of the "Word" Scriptures above. Write them out together and keep them in front of you. It's like putting puzzle pieces together. It helps us see the whole picture.

CHAPTER 12

"Desert Times"

Psalm 27 (MSG)
4 I'm asking God for one thing,
  only one thing:
  To live with him in his house
  my whole life long.
  I'll contemplate his beauty;
  I'll study at his feet.
8 When my heart whispered, "Seek God,"
  my whole being replied,
  "I'm seeking him!"
14 Stay with God!
  Take heart. Don't quit.
  I'll say it again:
  Stay with God.

MY FAVORITE CHRISTIAN preachers have taught me something empowering. I have learned from their sermons and their lives that the most life-changing message comes from a speaker who is preaching from their own struggles, faith, and breakthroughs.

I recently met with a friend of mine from church. She and her family have been through years of pain and disappointment due to an illness in their family. They have sought every answer medically and every miracle spiritually, but this lifelong illness remains unaffected. As I sat listening to her "stalemate" position with God, I was able to get heart-to-heart with her because even though my desert story looks different from hers, it still led me to the same dry, lifeless place.

I want to share with you the same thing I told her, "It's OK. God understands when we have nothing left to give. He sees our pain and He won't let go of us, even when we are ready to give up on Him."

One of the greatest testimonies I have from my walk with God is how He responds to my time of seeking Him. He shows up for me when I need Him most in amazing ways that go beyond anything I could ever ask of Him.

A few years ago I found myself in a three-and-a-half-year battle. Holding on to God through it all was the biggest test of faith I had ever faced. Month after month I sought God, believing that He would strengthen me and hopefully one day deliver me from it. I got to a place where I was battle weary and had no more reserves. I knew that this war was waged against me because I was on the path to fulfill God's vision for my life.

I was driving alone in my car during that time and found myself praying, "God, I have held on as long as I can. I have no more strength and my faith is dangerously weak. I've been in Your Word daily, praying it into my growing heart of faith, and in Your Word You've promised to be my strength. I need You to show up and fight for me." Within hours of my prayer Pastor Kumar, who at the time was one of the pastors at my church, called me. He said, "Debbie, I really need to talk to you." We set up a time to meet together in his office later that week. When I sat down in his office, he came around his desk and sat in a chair facing me. Leaning forward, with intensity in his eyes, he exclaimed, "Debbie, you are called to preach!" His statement left me in shock because I had only shared with a couple of my close friends the visions God had shown me. Kumar continued by saying, "There have been times in the past, such as when I saw you leading Kid's Church, that I've felt impressed about your calling, but this past Sabbath while you were ministering on the praise team, God impressed your call to preach so strongly in my heart that I knew I had to share it with you."

I sat there in awe as I realized that God was answering my prayer. He was confirming His vision for my life in a way that would not only get my attention, but also strengthen me to continue to believe and hold on. I absolutely love the way God does things. How He speaks and whom He speaks through is always over the top. Pastor Kumar even mentioned during our meeting that he's not the kind of person who walks around giving people messages from God. I have a lot of spiritual girlfriends who pray for me and encourage me all the time, but God knew that hearing from Him through Pastor Kumar, someone I don't usually hang out with or share my God-visions with, would really make me sit up and listen.

Another story that still amazes me whenever I think about it happened around that same time period. I had received an invitation to speak at a mother-daughter event at Washington Adventist University. My husband was out of town that week so I knew that I would be very busy keeping up with everything by myself. The Sunday before I spoke, I was roller-skating with one of my daughters and her friends. I was skating between them, holding their hands, when one of them fell suddenly, taking me down with her. I landed on my wrist and seriously injured it. So there I was, facing a very busy week ahead, needing time to prepare to speak, and now dealing with an injured wrist.

I couldn't use my wrist at all, so the next morning I had to ask my daughter Jasmine to help me put my shirt on when I got out of the shower. While we were standing in the bathroom she suddenly reached for her head, saying, "I feel really dizzy," then she hit the wall as she passed out! As I reached out with my good hand to try to help her up and make sure she was OK, I remember thinking, "What in the world is going on?!"

That whole week was a whirlwind. I prayed my way through each day, asking God what He had on His heart for me to speak to the group on Friday night, but I did not have a chance to sit down and write anything. Friday afternoon rolled around and I remember telling my girls, "I'm going to lock myself in the office with God and write down what He wants me to share tonight." I was so grateful when Jasmine responded by turning to her sister and saying, "Let's clean the house for Mom."

I went into my office, prayed, and then began to write what God spoke to me. On the way to my speaking engagement with my girls, we stopped to pick up Jasmine's boyfriend and his sister. As I waited in

DEBBIE HOWELL

my car for them to come out, their father, Ganoune, came to greet us. I told him where I was taking the kids and he said, "OK. If I have time I'll stop by and hear you speak."

The following week Ganoune called me. He said, "Debbie, you might not have seen me, but I came in late during your speaking engagement and I sat in the back as you were preaching. I don't know if you know what I do for a living, but I travel all over the world, training preachers. I've come to realize that there are two types of preachers: those who are trained and those who are called, and Debbie, I want to tell you that you are called to preach!" I almost fell out of my chair! I suddenly understood why there had been so many crazy attacks against me the previous week.

Can I just say something to you? I didn't learn this in a class or from reading a good book. This is my life talking to you. God will reward you as you earnestly seek Him. He is completely passionate about you. He wants more than anything to become the leading character in the story of your life. I pray that right now, as you read this book, that it will be as if I am sitting right next to you, pouring my encouragement and passion for God into your life.

Practicing the Word

Pick up your Bible and as you find God in its pages, ask the Holy Spirit to shed His light onto the words as you read them. Take time with each verse. One of my favorite things to do is to just find one verse, write it out, keep it in front of me for a week, and as I read it, ask the Holy Spirit to bring it to life within me.

CHAPTER 13

"The Word Made Flesh"

Psalm 27 (NCV)
4 I ask only one thing from the Lord.
This is what I want:
Let me live in the Lord's house
all my life.
Let me see the Lord's beauty
and look with my own eyes at his Temple.
8 My heart said of you, "Go, worship him."
So I come to worship you, Lord.
14 Wait for the Lord's help.
Be strong and brave,
and wait for the Lord's help.

"IN HIM WAS life, and the life was the light of all people." (John 1:4).

This is turning out to be a tough chapter for me to write. This last year God has begun to reveal some powerful Scriptures to me. There's so much He's been teaching me, but I fully recognize that my journey in His Word has only just begun.

Yesterday I looked up Scriptures on the Word, focusing mostly on powerful ones in John 1. I began to type the things that God has been teaching me, but felt overwhelmed and inadequate to bring all the pieces together. So I went back to my time with God. I picked up my journal where I've been writing down the Scriptures and book quotes that have inspired me and began to read them. I asked God for a greater anointing, fully recognizing that without His help, this book will not become a reality.

If you only take away one thing from this book, my prayer is that it will be this: You have to intentionally spend time with God in His Word to grow your faith. Living by faith means agreeing with and living according to Who He is and what He says in His Word. I can guarantee that as you set out to do that, He will respond in ways that will take your breath away! It may not happen that day or even that week, but if you are consistent in seeking His heart through His Word and His Spirit, He will reward you.

I was rewarded this morning. Instead of giving into the feelings I had of being inept to write this book, I chose to sit with God and grow my faith by reading out loud things like this prayer that I journaled from Psalm 119:27, "Make me understand what Your precepts mean so I can tell others of Your wonderful way."

When I woke up this morning, I picked up a book to read and the first thing I saw was a Scripture. As I began reading it, I recognized immediately that God was answering my prayer and responding to my faith. "See, the Lord your God has given you the land. Go up and take possession of it as the Lord, the God of your ancestors, told you. Do not be afraid; do not be discouraged." (Deuteronomy 1:21). I wish I could describe to you the amazing depth of feeling that comes when God speaks through His Word. They aren't just words on a page anymore. They are the very breath of God, through His Spirit, that penetrates my heart and brings me to my knees in worship.

You see, through this Scripture God was confirming to me that I'm on the right path by writing this book. It's the "land He's already promised me." All I need to do is step forward in faith and possess it. My enemies are fear and discouragement, and the way to defeat them is to stand in faith that my "land," (this book) has already been written in Heaven, I just have to claim it here on earth.

"It was Jesus' words that brought life to the world. His words drove out demons and healed diseases. His words calmed storms and raised the dead. Our whole Bible is filled with His words and those words have power. Jesus wanted to build His followers' faith in the Scriptures. When He was gone, those words would have to be their source of faith and power... We should study the Bible carefully, asking for the help of the Holy Spirit to understand it... The promises and prayers found there are meant for us personally. Eating the bread from Heaven means absorbing the words of God in the Bible — applying those words to our own lives until they change our character" (Jerry D. Thomas, "Messiah"). See John 6:35.

"Jesus said to Peter, 'I will give you the keys of the kingdom of Heaven.' These keys were the words of Jesus Himself, both as He walked this earth and as written in the books of Scripture. Those who share these powerful words open the doors of Heaven to all who will believe." ("Messiah").

In the New Testament John began his book by saying, "In the beginning was the Word, and the Word was with God, and the Word was God. He was with God in the beginning. Through him all things were made; without him nothing was made that was made... The Word became flesh and made his dwelling among us. We have seen his glory, the glory of the one and only Son, who came from the Father, full of grace and truth."

The Voice version of the Bible does something very interesting. It replaces "word" with "voice." I want to share some verses from John chapter 1 taken from this version.

"The Voice was and is God... This celestial Word remained ever present with the Creator; His speech shaped the entire cosmos. Immersed in the practice of creating, all things that exist were birthed in Him. His breath filled all things with a living, breathing light — a light that thrives in the depths of darkness, blazes through murky bottoms. It cannot and will not be quenched.

"The Voice took on flesh and became human and chose to live alongside us. We have seen Him, enveloped in undeniable splendor — the one true Son of the Father — evidenced in the perfect balance of grace and truth... God, unseen until now, is revealed in the Voice, God's only Son, straight from the Father's heart."

These words reveal to us the power of the Word in creation, then continue by revealing the fact that God wrapped flesh around the Word and sent Him to earth where He was given the name "Jesus." Here He continued to work His creative power by speaking His Father's heart, His very Word.

For me, the one story above all others that reveals Jesus as the Word of creation is the resurrection of Lazarus. I think some of us have heard that story so many times that it has lost its significance for us. Sit back with me for a moment and use your imagination to step into this story. Lazarus had been dead for *three* days. His body had been prepared, wrapped, and shut away in a dark, cold tomb. The funeral service was done, mourners had come and gone, and his friends and family had said their goodbyes. It was done, finished, final.

Now into the story steps the Word, the Voice, the creative power of God! All of a sudden death came face to face with the power of light and life. The power of death was no match for the miraculous power of Jesus. The reality and finality of death couldn't stay the same when Jesus *spoke life*! What had been devoid of life suddenly stepped out of the tomb with new life and vitality! Do you see why I get excited about planting the Word of God into my life? The Word we hold in our hands, together with the power of the Holy Spirit, has been given to us to bring the same light and life to the dark places of the world today! (Thoughts borrowed from a powerful sermon I once heard from T.D. Jakes).

Practicing the Word

In "The Bush is Still Burning," Lloyd John Ogilvie writes, "Jesus is none other than Yahweh, the creative word of God... He is truth about God's essential being for us to behold and know." (pp. 18-19)

Jesus has called us to be the voice behind Scripture. After He returned to Heaven, His disciples continued bringing salvation and healing by speaking the words and Name of Jesus.

We need to practice being the voice behind God's Word. Find a recording app on your phone. Every morning record yourself reading a Scripture (it could be just one verse) and play it back to listen to throughout the day. As the verses are planted in your heart through this process, your faith will grow as you begin to believe in what God is saying to you.

Here are some to get you started:

"Now I, with unveiled face, look at Christ to see His brightness reflected in the mirror of the Word of God." (2 Corinthians 3:18)

"Jesus came that I may have life, and have it abundantly." (John 10:10, adapted)

"Let the morning bring me word of your unfailing love, for I have put my trust in you. Show me the way I should go, for to you I entrust my life." (Psalm 143:8, NIV)

"Jesus, I thank you that you live in my heart through faith and that I am rooted and established in your love." (Ephesians 3:17, NIV, adapted)

DEBBIE HOWELL

CHAPTER 14

"Agreeing With God"

Psalm 27 (VOICE)
4 I am pleading with the Eternal for this one thing,
    my soul's desire:
    To live with Him all of my days—
    in the shadow of His temple,
    To behold His beauty and ponder His ways
    in the company of His people.
8 The prodding of my heart leads me to chase after You.
    I am seeking You, Eternal One—don't retreat from me.
9 You have always answered my call.
14 Please answer me: Don't give up.
    Wait for the Eternal in expectation, and be strong.
    Again, wait for the Eternal.

"THE LAW OF God is an expression of His very nature; it is an embodiment of the great principle of love, and hence is the foundation of His government in Heaven and earth...When the principle of love is implanted in the heart, when man is renewed after the image of Him that created him, the new-covenant promise is fulfilled, 'I will put my laws into their hearts, and in their minds will I write them.'" Hebrews 10:16 (Ellen G. White - Steps to Christ, p. 39)

The process of knowing God through His Word is relationship-based. Because of that, trust is a key element in connecting with God through praying His Word back to Him. There are many things that can block us from making the decision to seek God, and lack of trust is one that is very common. Our lack of trust can have many different faces. Not trusting God to provide for us, not trusting that He will protect us, not trusting that He cares enough to bother with us and our situations, not trusting that what He has to offer is more amazing and exciting than what He is asking us to give up.

I want to address this issue because it is so important that we face our fears (lack of trust) head on and begin embracing the indescribable relationship with God that Jesus died to give us.

To illustrate this point I want to share something that happened to me just a few days ago. My husband, Chris, and I spent three days and two nights out on a boat in the Great Barrier Reef in Australia to go snorkeling and diving. He planned this amazing trip for us to celebrate our 26th wedding anniversary. We were both excited and felt so blessed that we were able to do this together. We have done many missions trips to the islands of Micronesia, starting in 1986, so we have enjoyed numerous snorkeling opportunities together. But he's a certified diver; I am not. Because we were going to be diving in one of the "seven wonders of the world" he signed me up for three introductory dives. Having never taken a diving class, I was thrilled that I would be able to go with the help of a certified instructor.

One problem: I have this fear of being trapped under water. It's been a fear of mine for years because I got trapped under the water a couple of times as a child and thought I was going to drown. I've confirmed, even embraced this fear every time I've seen a movie clip that showed someone trapped under water. My immediate thought is always the same, "If I were an actress I could *never* do that scene!" I knew that diving would be a challenge for me, but I was totally unprepared for how strong my fear would fight against me.

I had arranged to go on a dive with one of the instructors on our first day out. I got into the water with him and a "second time" student. As he began to guide me under the water I could feel my panic rising. Every time he would start to take me below the surface I would fight and pop my head back up. Finally the guide looked at me and said, "Once you trust me and your equipment you will be OK." He then lowered us into the water, looked me in the face and gave me the sign to watch him. Then he adjusted my mask and made sure everything was in place. As we began our dive he held onto me and guided me from behind so I didn't feel alone. I focused on relaxing and began watching the beautiful fish as they swam around us. I don't even know how to describe what happened next. The only way I can explain it is that all of a sudden the fear that I was working to conquer returned to the battle with a new strategic plan called "Panic." Without warning, I felt like I couldn't breathe and instinctively I pulled out my breathing regulator. My guide tried to put it back in my mouth but I wouldn't let him. The next few moments entailed him pulling me back up to the surface, and I felt that I was living out my lifelong fear — being unable to breathe under water. Now, in reality, we weren't deep enough for me to have drowned. Not under the supervision of my certified guide. However, in my mind, I was living my last moments on this earth.

My panic was so overwhelming by this point that I opted to swim back to the boat instead of facing my fear again. Back on the boat, I spent a lot of time processing what had happened and wondering how I was going to do better for my next dive. I talked with Chris about it. He was surprised at how panic-stricken I was over diving. He knows that I am not a fearful person by nature. I love adventure and I can handle most common fears such as heights, mice, spiders, and snakes. But all he would have to do was to start talking about diving and he could literally see the fear take hold of me. My eyes would get big and I would start shaking. He said, "It's mind over matter. You can't listen to your fears."

My game plan was to try my second dive on our second day on the boat. In the meantime I went snorkeling several times and relaxed, in awe of God's creation. That night we were sleeping in our cabin and all of a sudden at 3 a.m. I woke up with about 573 knots in my stomach. My fear had literally woken me up so that I could obsess about diving! I tried to calm myself down, but my fear would not be distracted. I was anxious about it all through that morning, and it didn't help matters at all when I found out a few hours later that the intro diving class for that day was so full that I would have to wait another day to go. So after another full day of snorkeling I went to bed, only to have another restless night of sleep. I remember thinking to myself, "This is totally ridiculous. I'm going on a shallow dive. I'm with a certified instructor. Even the sign about this class states that it's fun, safe, and easy." I was also frustrated with myself because I was determined that I was not going to leave the Great Barrier Reef without going on a dive.

On our third and final day on the boat, I set my mind to face my fear, no matter what. I had found some powerful Scriptures to hold on to such as:

> "So you don't need to tremble in fear. I'll tell you what My plans are for you." (Isaiah 44:8, Prayer Bible, A Modern Translation)

> "I am the Lord your God. I, the Lord of the heavens, cause ocean waves to roar. I have told you what to say, and you are safe in My hand. I set all the stars in place and I created the earth, and I say to Israel, 'You are mine.'" (Isaiah 51:15–16, Prayer Bible)

What's funny is that my fear had me so convinced that I would die if I tried diving, that I found myself reminding God that He has given me a vision for my life and therefore He needed to make sure I didn't drown!

I had signed up to go on a dive with a class on our final day. Somehow in packing up our luggage and taking it out of our cabin I missed the announcement that the class was leaving, so I was too late to join them. As a last ditch effort to face my lifelong fear, I talked one of the instructors into taking me out. After two days of feeling anxious, God had the perfect plan for me. I went out with two instructors and Chris. With the three of them watching out for me and being patient with me I was able to complete my very first dive! Chris helped me feel calm by regularly reminding me to breathe in and out slowly. Having him with me made all the difference. It was so incredible to go down and watch as schools of fish swam around us. I can't believe that I almost let fear steal that experience from me!

It is just incredible how closely my diving story mirrors what I'm passionate about sharing with you. We have to get to the place where we refuse to listen to our fears and frustrations regarding God. We can spend our whole lives digging our own holes of defeat by what we think and what we say to ourselves. It's "mind over matter" because the battle is waging itself in your mind. (Joyce Meyer wrote a great book on this called "Battlefield of the Mind.")

God has so much He wants to say to you; so much to bless you with, so much He wants to pour into your life. We all have that "thing" that keeps us from stepping out into the water and believing that with Him we are safe. With Him we will go on the journey of a lifetime. We are so afraid to give up what we know and what we think makes us happy. We stubbornly hold on to past hurts, sins, and failures, not believing that God is bigger than all of that.

When the guide on my first dive looked at me and said, "When you trust me and your equipment you will be okay," he got my attention. That's exactly what God is saying to us right now. "When you learn to trust Me and what I've equipped you with (The Bible and the Holy Spirit), you will be ready to go into deep waters with Me. Letting go and slipping into unknown territory is frightening. I have a new respect for fear and for people who deal with fear and anxiety on a regular basis. It's the real deal. I'm sitting here shaking my head, just remembering what a powerful force it was over me.

God knows that the enemy loves to paralyze us with fear. I heard a preacher once say that God says 365 times in the Bible "Do not fear." That's one for every day of the year. God equipped us with enough promises to keep us strong despite our fears.

Practicing the Word

It is essential as we get to know God through His Word, that we get our minds over the "matter" of our realities by speaking God's Words of life over ourselves. One thing that I've discovered about tapping into the power of Scripture is the beauty of putting Scriptures together as a prayer. I encourage you to write down this example and then write some of your own. You can find many Scriptures to choose from by going to *Biblegateway.com*.

"Lord, I wait patiently for You; listen to me and hear my request. You brought me up out of a horrible pit. You set me on a rock and established my life. You put a new song in my heart, even praise to You for delivering me. Many will hear my song of worship to You; they, too, will put their trust in You." (Psalm 40:1–3, Prayer Bible) "I will walk close beside you; Your strong right hand will steady me." (Psalm 64:8) "God, You are love… There is no fear in love… Your perfect love drives out my fear." (1 John 4:16–18, adapted) "Teach me your way, Lord, that I may rely on your faithfulness; give me an undivided heart, that I may fear your name." (Psalm 86:11, NIV)

As powerful as these verses are, the connection they make with your story begins when you pray and ask the Holy Spirit to speak to you through them. It takes time, but hearing the voice of God through His Spirit revealing His Words to our hearts is the goal we are after.

CHAPTER 15

"Living Inspired"

Psalm 27 (WYC)

4 I asked of the Lord one thing; I shall seek this thing; that I dwell in the house of the Lord all the days of my life. That I see the will of the Lord; and that I visit his temple. (I asked of the Lord only one thing; and I shall seek this thing; that I live in the House of the Lord all the days of my life. So that I can see the beauty of the Lord; and I can seek his guidance in his Temple.)

8 Mine heart said to thee, My face sought thee; Lord, I shall seek again thy face. (And thou saidest, Seek ye my face; and my heart said to thee, Lord, I shall seek thy face.)

14 Abide thou the Lord, do thou manly; and thine heart be comforted, and suffer thou the Lord. (Wait thou for the Lord, be thou encouraged; let thy heart be strengthened, and wait thou for the Lord.)

IF YOU AND I ever had the privilege of meeting and chatting together, there would be certain things on my heart to share with you. Top on my list would be the truth that from the moment God created you, He planted an amazing dream and purpose into your DNA.

The Bible is full of incredible stories of men and women who stepped forward to release the power of God into the world around them. To read their stories, enlightened by the Holy Spirit's leading, stirs a desire deep within me to follow their paths, which began at the very heart of God, into the realm of living the impossible for His glory.

Not only would I take the time to tell you that there is a God-vision planted deep within you that begs to be realized and lived out, but I would reveal to you the secrets I'm discovering on how to stay strong and empowered for that journey with Him.

It's all about tapping into Who God is and how His stories are played out through the lives of His people. Time reading and praying through His Word is without a doubt the most essential thing to do. Aside from my personal reading and prayer time, soaking in the ministry of God's modern-day spiritual giants is another thing that also keeps me "fired up" in my faith, believing that God desires and is able to do the impossible through me. When I read testimonies by T.D. Jakes, Jim Cymbala, Mark Batterson, and Holley Gerth; when I hear the anointing on Joyce Meyer's sermons or Darlene Zschech's worship songs, I am encouraged to know that God, even today, is choosing to do His greatest work through the lives of broken people.

Broken people. God loves to step into the stories of broken people. There's something about brokenness that gets God's attention. I know from more than one experience that the times God has used me the most powerfully, the times when His anointing has been tangible in my life, have been when I've had to press through my brokenness to speak, or to pray, or to sing. I've heard before that we all have times in life when we have to face fear. The key to defeating fear when responding to God's purpose for your life is to "do it afraid." Let me take it a step further and say that God sometimes calls us at the most inopportune moments. If He is calling you to do something at the very moment you feel broken, then just "do it broken."

God's Word comes to life in new ways for us when we feel like failures. Earlier today I found a treasure in Psalm 33. Worshipping God is one of my favorite things to do, so these verses got my attention: "Lord, I rejoice because You allow me to approach You; I worship You as I come to You... I write new songs of worship to You; I sing praises to You from the bottom of my heart... You spoke and the hemisphere just appeared...Everything You spoke was done just like You said; everything happened just as You wanted it to happen." (Prayer Bible, Psalm 33)

Wow! Did you catch the last part of that Scripture? If you read the whole chapter, it refers to God as the God of creation and how everything God spoke at creation happened just as He planned it — just as He said it would. You see, the broken part of me could easily be talked out of doing what I do for God, even writing this book. I could look at myself, my inadequacies, my failures, my lack of pretty much everything I need for my God-vision. But, when I sit with God in His Word, something outside of myself, something eternal and holy steps into the picture and I find myself believing in the God of creation, the God of the impossible.

In the very beginning of the Bible, God spoke His power at creation, and starting with light, called forth everything from nothing. Then, in the first four chapters of the New Testament Jesus steps into the picture and brings the power of Heaven to earth by speaking the same power of creation — God's power through His Word. Starting in Acts, Jesus' followers joined in and realized the same miracles by the same power — Jesus' Name and the Word of God. So when I read Scriptures that declare things like, "The Word of God is flawless." (Proverbs 30:5) "The Word of God endures forever." (Isaiah 40:8) "No Word from God will never fail." (Luke 1:37) I begin to think outside the box of my human limitations. I realize that God is calling me to the next chapter of His story in history. It's not through my talent or self-confidence that I believe, it's through my brokenness and growing intimacy with God that I have faith to step out of what *I* know into what *God* knows — His Word. I know that God's Word is just as powerful today as it was in Genesis, John, and Acts.

Here's an example that just came to me. My husband, Chris, can put together and fix just about anything. The fact that "opposites attract" is my excuse for not being able to assemble or repair even the simplest of projects. I remember trying once to put together a bookcase by myself and I literally assembled it upside down *and* backward. So let's say that Chris bought me a brand new TV and blue ray DVD player. What I have received has the potential of bringing something awesome into my life, but if it's not configured or plugged in properly it won't do me any good. I could sit for days looking at the directions (whether it's written in English or Chinese doesn't matter — it's all Greek to me!) trying to figure out where in the world all of those wires are supposed to go. But all I would have to do is give Chris my "pathetic, defeated face" and he would set it up and show me how to operate it.

The Bible and the presence of the Holy Spirit are more than gifts for us. They are the promise of the power of God to be realized here on earth. When we ask the Holy Spirit to plug us into the power of God's Word, His presence will become a reality in our lives. I have just begun to realize that in my own life that even the baby steps I'm taking with God, His Word, and His Spirit have led to amazing things happening. I will share one of those stories in my next chapter.

Practicing the Word

Sometimes finding time for God is only half of the battle. The other half can be finding a quiet place to meet with Him. In the recently released movie, "War Room," the characters set up prayer rooms in closets where they posted prayers on the wall as they wrote and prayed them. If you have an extra closet or corner in your home, this would be a great use of the space. Otherwise, try to find a special room in your home where you can comfortably sit and keep your Bible and journal near. It's even nice to hang something inspirational in that area. Once you become comfortable in this special place with God in His Word, you will find it easier to disconnect from distractions and focus on His presence.

CHAPTER 16

"Christianity and Kangaroo Burgers"

Psalm 27 (KJV)

4 One thing have I desired of the Lord, that will I seek after;
that I may dwell in the house of the Lord all the days of
my life, to behold the beauty of the Lord, and to enquire
in his temple.

8 When thou saidst, Seek ye my face; my heart said unto
thee, Thy face, Lord, will I seek.

14 Wait on the Lord: be of good courage, and he shall
strengthen thine heart: wait, I say, on the Lord.

MY HUSBAND AND I are more than halfway through
our month-long trip to Australia. During our time here
we have met a lot of incredible people. Australians are some of the
most hospitable people we've ever met. They know how to fully enjoy
quality time eating, talking, and laughing. They also know how to grill
kangaroo meat and make tasty kangaroo burgers! That was definitely
one of our "cultural" moments.

We were invited to a barbecue (what Australians call a "Barbie")
a couple of nights ago. During our time with our new friends, Chris
and I mentioned that the next morning we were planning to visit the
Hillsong Church in their area.

That comment led to a discussion where people opened up about
their experiences with God and church, and a few of them said, "I really
need to start going to church again. Maybe I will join you." As I fell
asleep that night, I found myself praying that the Holy Spirit would

move mightily on their behalf. When I woke up the next morning I continued to pray for them, and I also picked up the "Messiah" book I had been reading. I was totally amazed when I read, "Jesus has on occasion directed His followers to a certain house on a certain street in a certain city to find one of His lost sheep." Being inspired by that I thought, "I need to find a Scripture to pray over them in my heart as we go to church today." I opened up my Bible and my eyes fell to a text that I had underlined. The text said, "Invite everyone to look to Me for salvation. I am God, and there is no other; what I have said will come true. Everyone will bow down and worship Me." (Isaiah 45:22-24, The Prayer Bible, A Modern Translation) I was in awe of how clearly God was speaking to me! I shared all of this with Chris and together in our hotel room we prayed that God would reach our new friends.

One of our friends picked us up and took us to Hillsong Church. We arrived early, so we had time to stand in the church foyer before the service started. As we were waiting there, one of the church members came over to me and said, "Hi. I recognize you. It's great to see you again. Who's your friend?" As I introduced our friend I was thinking, "That's weird, I've never been here before." The church member then proceeded to take our friend over to a booth and came back shortly after with a glowing smile and said, "Your friend just signed up to join one of our small groups. What is so great is that she is Kiwi [from New Zealand] and the leader of our group is also Kiwi!"

A few minutes later our friend walked back toward us with tears in her eyes. She was sensing that God was reaching out to her through the beautiful members of Hillsong. Wow! The service hadn't even started yet and God was already fulfilling what He said He would do.

There are so many ways and places God is longing to release His power, but He is waiting for us to grow in a relationship with Him that will produce faith in His Word. That faith will then release His power through His Word into this world!

I am blessed to be part of a Christian radio show called "Fresh Start" with my incredible friend, Renée (*http://briteradio.org/fresh-start.html*) One day during a break, Cliff, a radio voice from another show, threw me a curveball. He said, "Debbie, you need to write a book. What you share on your radio show about praying Scripture is very powerful, but most of us don't know how to do it." In a polite, but sarcastic way I said, "Okay. Yeah, sure."

God was opening a door, but I didn't recognize it yet. After that day He put people in my path to get my attention. There were two different people in two separate encounters who said the same thing: "It's Okay to pray, but don't get your hopes up. God may not answer you." Something deep within me was unleashed as I heard those comments. It was a sort of righteous indignation as I thought, "How can God answer the prayers of His people when we feel defeated even before we pray?" A great desire began to grow in me; a desire to share with the world what God has been teaching me. Our lack of faith is directly related to our lack of knowing God through His Word and not embracing the Holy Spirit's presence in our lives.

As I set out to write this book, God continued to show up in unexpected ways in His predetermined timing to grow my faith. Last month I listened as Christian movie producer, Alex Kendrick, gave the most powerful testimony I've ever heard. I was at a local church with my 14-year-old daughter, Camilia, and some of our friends from Brite Radio. We were riveted during his entire talk (even Camilia soaked in every word!). Alex began at the very beginning of his journey with God as God called him way out of his comfort zone and into the vision He had for his life. As I sat there listening to the powerful, yet humorous ways God did the impossible with each Christian movie Alex and his team filmed, that "still, small voice" deep within me stirred my faith and said, "If God did that for Alex, there's nothing He won't do for you..."

God's timing was perfect, since at the time I was just days from boarding a plane to head to Australia for a month, where I would have plenty of time to write. Hearing Alex's miraculous stories left me with a "sitting-on-the-edge-of-my-seat" excitement, waiting and wondering what this journey with God would look like. I've loved every moment I've had with God so far, and every day His Spirit inspires me with what to write, but the miracles I need are just getting started. Daily I'm releasing my faith that God will provide the editor and publisher of His choosing. The "unknowns" can leave us scared and uncertain, or as we choose to sit with God every day, it can be the most amazing adventure with Him!

Practicing the Word

Like me, if you are ready to see more of God's power flow through your life, then it's time to release your faith. God already has the power, His Word has already spoken His presence into our lives. What's left to be realized is our faith to take hold of it. It's time to be bold. If you haven't started writing in a journal yet, *now* is the time to do it. Begin writing and praying God's Word and presence over yourself. I've shared some of my favorites to get you started.

> "Father, I pray that You will strengthen, complete, and perfect me; that You will make me what I should be; that You will equip me with everything good to carry out Your will while You work in me and accomplish what is pleasing in Your sight." (Hebrews 13:20–21, adapted)

> "In God I live, and move, and have my being." (Acts 17:26–28, adapted)

> "The Word [spoken by] Christ has its home [in my heart and mind]. It dwells in me in [all its] riches… Whatever I do [no matter what it is] in word or deed, I do everything in the name of the Lord Jesus." (Colossians 3, adapted)

> "I thank You, God, that through Christ I can spread the fragrant knowledge of You." (2 Corinthians 2:14)

CHAPTER 17

"We Wish to See Jesus" (John 11:20–28)

Psalm 27 (NET Bible)
4 I have asked the Lord for one thing—
  this is what I desire!
  I want to live in the Lord's house all the days of my life,
  so I can gaze at the splendor of the Lord
  and contemplate in his temple.
8 My heart tells me to pray to you,
  and I do pray to you, O Lord.
14 Rely on the Lord!
  Be strong and confident!
  Rely on the Lord!

IT'S THE CRY of our hearts. It's why we continue to believe in prayer even when it doesn't seem to work for us. It's why we believe in the Bible even if in our own lives it's not alive and full of power. When every distraction in our lives is stripped away, what's left in each of our hearts is, "We wish to see Jesus."

It would have been so amazing to walk and talk with Jesus while He lived on this earth. It almost seems like the disciples had an unfair advantage over us as we struggle to know Jesus as they did. My whole attitude about that changed recently as I heard a preacher say, "Just as Jesus walked and talked with His disciples and they were drawn into intimacy with God through Him, we have the privilege to know God's heart by His presence on earth through the ministry of the Holy Spirit."

That statement has fueled the journey I'm on this year as I study and embrace the ministry of the Holy Spirit.

Author Lloyd John Ogilvie has often inspired me through his powerful books. In "The Bush is Still Burning" he writes, "He is here. He knows me and I know Him. It is no figure of speech; it is the realest thing in the world." That's the prayer of my heart. I wish to see Jesus through the mirror of God's Word and the presence of the Holy Spirit in my life. In another one of his books Ogilvie talks about how as Christians we accept Christ through baptism and the seal of the Holy Spirit. I was baptized at the age of 13 and I've been to a lot of baptisms, but have never heard about the importance of being sealed by the Holy Spirit as the next step. As I study about it I realize that not only is it biblical, but Jesus Himself, was sealed with the Holy Spirit after His baptism, and as our example, it's something we need to follow.

Without the seal — the presence of the Holy Spirit in our lives — our walk with God becomes frustrating because we can't live as God tells us to live, and the Bible has no holy or eternal meaning for us. I have to smile as I think back to my baptism. My decision to become baptized came from deep within my heart. I was ready to give my life fully to God and was so blessed to have my Uncle Bob baptize me. In my young mind I had a plan. I learned through my baptismal studies that when I went under the surface to be baptized, Jesus would wash away all my sins, and as I rose up out of the water God would give me a clean slate. I was determined to do it right, to make the most of my new life and not fall into sin again. Imagine my feelings of failure when the very day after my baptism I lost my temper and yelled at my sister!

Living united with God through His Spirit begins with two easy steps. Invite Him into your life and whenever He speaks, obey. A great time to start this journey with Him is when you begin to read your Bible. Ask Him to put an anointing on your time with Him and believe that He will speak the heart of God to you through His Word.

DEBBIE HOWELL

Practicing the Word

Find a quiet place. If your home is full of kids, love, and noise then maybe the best option is to go outside and sit in your yard or car for a few moments. Once you find your space with God, take time to pray this prayer:

Father I believe that You are pouring Your love into my heart through the Holy Spirit. I receive the presence, joy, and peace of the Holy Spirit into my life. Because You promised us the Holy Spirit and I am inviting His presence into my life, I have now received His Spirit, which will connect me with Your heart and open my eyes to Your Word. Amen. (Based on Romans 5:5; 15:13.)

CHAPTER 18

"Awakened to His Word"

Psalm 27 (NLT)
4 The one thing I ask of the Lord—
   the thing I seek most—
   is to live in the house of the Lord all the days of my life,
   delighting in the Lord's perfections
   and meditating in his Temple.
8 My heart has heard you say, "Come and talk with me."
   And my heart responds, "Lord, I am coming."
14 Wait patiently for the Lord.
   Be brave and courageous.
   Yes, wait patiently for the Lord.

I FIND IT very interesting how little Jesus' disciples understood the things that He said while He lived with them. Even when Jesus spoke plainly with them they just didn't understand Him or His kingdom. I see some similarities in today's frustrations as we try our "best" to live as Christians. We can live under the "Christian" label and say that we believe in Jesus, but that alone won't enable us to live a Christ-like life.

Since the second half of the Bible is about Jesus' life and the lives of His followers, it's important that we learn about His life. Today I was reading about Jesus in the book "Messiah," and God gave me a revelation. In this particular story Jesus is getting ready to enjoy a meal with His disciples, and as was customary for that time, they were waiting to have their dusty feet washed. The water, basin, and towels were ready for them, but there was no servant to perform this undesirable task. As Jesus looked around the room, He realized that the disciples were too proud to do this servant's job. The author then poses this question: "How could He awaken the love in their hearts that would make them understand His words?" That question hit deep in my heart. The whole premise of this book is how to know God, how to pray, and how to hear from Him in His Word. This question became an answer for me. You can't really "get" God's Word, His purpose, or His kingdom unless you have a revelation of His love in your heart. During this story the disciples were so consumed and distracted by their thoughts of who would become the greatest in Jesus' earthly kingdom that they missed an opportunity to serve — to understand Jesus' Words through loving others.

So, once again, Jesus leads by example. Going around the table He washes, loves, and ministers to 24 dusty feet and 12 proud hearts. The love that shone through His heart of humility that day made such an impact that the author writes, "Jesus wanted to wash the jealousy and pride out of their hearts. Without an attitude of humility and love, they were not ready to share the memorial service Jesus was about to create. But by washing their feet, Jesus created this change. Except for Judas, their hearts were united with love for each other and each was ready for someone else to have the most important position. Now they were ready to listen and learn." (Messiah)

God's kingdom is based on love. God so loved the world that He gave Jesus. Jesus so loved the world that He gave Himself. The Holy Spirit's passion is to connect us with God's heart of love. Love is the key that opens the door for us to know God through His Word and through prayer. I remember being moved by God's heart of love one day a few years ago. I had set aside some time to spend with Him and from a place deep within my heart I felt God call me to minister His love. He said, "Debbie, pour your heart and soul out for My people." I didn't know exactly how that was to be played out, but it was such a profound moment for me that I took a huge step of faith and responded, "Yes God, whatever that looks like, I promise to do it."

I'm still figuring out what that will ultimately look like. I've made a lot of mistakes along the way, but because of His grace I have been able to walk through every door He's opened and give my all for Him.

I didn't know that the doors would lead to having a Christian morning radio show with my dear friend Renée, or that I would be led to write this book. I have no clue what all of my tomorrows will look like, but I am determined to fulfill God's call on my life. The only way I can achieve that is to follow the passion I have for God's heart through His Word. It is my prayer that this book will spark that same desire for you.

Practicing the Word

There is no right or wrong way to begin your journey to God's heart through His Word. God will reward your time and efforts. I want to encourage you to write this prayer out and pray it every day. It's based on the Scriptures that I shared in Chapter 11. Remember that what you say and what you believe are important in this process, so start your day by confessing prayers like this one.

Father, Your Word is very near me; it's in my mouth and in my heart. When I speak Your Words they carry Your Spirit and life. As I accept instruction from Your mouth and lay up Your Words in my heart, my faith grows in Your promise that none of Your Words will ever fail. It will not return to You empty, but will accomplish what You desire. Thank You, God, that Your Word is alive and active in my life as You are watching to see that it is fulfilled. Amen.

ONE THING I ASK...

Made in the
USA
Columbia, SC